One Trip Around the Sun

MEENA,
ENJOY THE TRIP!

One Trip Around the Sun

A Guide To Using
Diet Herbs, Exercise, and Meditation
to Harmonize with the Seasons

Rory Lipsky, L.Ac.

RiverWood Books
ASHLAND, OREGON

Printed in Malaysia

First edition: 2003

06 05 04 03   9 8 7 6 5 4 3 2 1

Cover design by David Ruppe

Library of Congress Cataloging-in-Publication Data

Lipsky, Rory.
  One trip around the sun : a guide to using diet herbs, exercise, and
meditation to harmonize with the seasons / Rory Lipsky.-- 1st American
pbk. ed.
     p. cm.
Includes index.
  ISBN 1-883991-85-4 (paperback)
  1. Medicine, Chinese. 2. Seasons. I. Title.
  R601.L679 2003
  613--dc22
                          2003016017

Table of Contents

Acknowledgments

This book is dedicated to all people who seek to live a harmonious life. It is also dedicated to anyone who dreams of publishing their work, it can be done!

I would like to thank my parents David and Sheila, and my new parents Dick and Jasminka, my grandparents, my brother Bret, my sister Christy, my new brothers Eric (thank you for the illustrations) and Teddy, My Aunt Teri and Uncle Leonard, My Aunt Linda and Uncle Vic, Angela Lipsky and all my friends and family who have been so loving and supportive.

I would like to thank all my Martial Arts, Chi Kung, and Meditation teachers, especially Bruce Eichelberger and Carl Totton.

I would like to thank all my Acupuncture, Chinese Medicine and bodywork Teachers.

I would especially like to thank my loving wife Avril who supports all my dreams and visions, and encourages me to pursue them with my full vigor.

This book is a dream-come true for me and it is my intention that it empowers all those who read it.

Vitality For All!

Basic Concepts

Introduction

*J*OHN, WHO IS THIRTY-THREE, would not call himself a rock star, but he is one. When he first came to me for help, he was in intense physical and psychological pain. "I'm going mental," was the way he put it. In terms of traditional Chinese medicine, I could see that parts of his body — especially his hands, forearms, and back — were energetically blocked. The stress of his career was clearly taking a toll.

Involved in creating music, photos, graphics, and stories, he was intensely emotional and accustomed to channeling his powerful feelings into his art. He enjoyed expressing himself in a variety of art forms. My challenge was to help him release his blockages without interfering with his amazing creative flow.

John has a unique way of seeing the world and a tremendous amount of energy flowing through his body. He has a wide-ranging, inquisitive mind and throws himself passionately into whatever he does. Although the intensity of his involvement sometimes makes him feel crazy, it seems to have done no permanent damage. Interacting with negative aspects of his experience is part of his pattern. "When I talk about the negative," he told me, "I get a little nuts."

Because of John's career demands and lifestyle, he could not schedule acupuncture and bodywork sessions on a regular schedule. Sometimes we would work four times a week, but other times he would go for weeks without treatment.

I put him on a regimen of Chinese herbs, which he continued taking even during our hiatus periods, and he reported some significant changes. "I just feel cleaner and lighter," he said. "It's like the juice goes through me much smoother. The work we do is killer."

I still work with John, and while his life has become even more demanding with his growing success, the herbal approach he uses allows him to stay more grounded while keeping his creative energy flowing.

Even though I'm very familiar with Chinese medicine, I'm continually amazed by the dramatic effects this ancient approach to health has on the lives of my clients. They come with a wide variety of problems, and it's a privilege to help some who remind me of myself as a troubled young man.

Growing up, I often felt isolated; by the time I was a teenager, loneliness was a prevalent force in my life. Continually battling depression, I had no idea what was going on with me psychologically, and I had no skills to communicate my feelings. These troubles manifested in poor schoolwork, rebelliousness, and severe mood swings. I assumed this pattern was something I would just have to live with.

My college roommate was immersed in Taoism, which I found fascinating. For the first time I saw the possibility of relief from my inner turmoil. I began practicing meditation and *chi kung* and reading books on Taoist philosophy. The spiritual awakening I found in Taoism was a turning point in my life. I realized that what I had gone through growing up was necessary, that it motivated me to search for something deeper in life. I realized that there is an intelligent force flowing through all creation, and that I could align myself with it.

When the school year ended, I went home and began an apprenticeship at a Chinese herb shop. There I learned the basics of Chinese medicine in a practical way and saw how the medicine affected the lives of actual people. I also found a martial arts school that focused on Taoist practices. I began practicing chi kung, martial arts, and meditation. By the end of that summer, I had a clearer understanding of what I

4

wanted to do with my life: I wanted to learn to heal myself and help others do the same. Instead of going back to college, I continued working at the herb shop and studying martial arts. I also enrolled in a massage therapy program.

After getting my massage therapy certification, I began working with clients. I performed massage and recommended herbs, but after about a year I realized I needed more knowledge, so I went to acupuncture school. By the time I began my internship in clinical acupuncture practice, I was reaping huge benefits from my prior training. My practices of meditation, chi kung, and massage gave me an intuitive freedom with my acupuncture patients, so my sessions offered far more than just the insertion of needles. I learned to blend my skills into a unique style of practice.

My sessions today involve acupuncture, subtle energy work, and deep tissue bodywork. By combining these modalities in one session, I can work on a variety of levels, from the subtle to the physical. This way helps to integrate the different aspects of a patient, and the channeling of refined subtle energy provides a supportive flow that's especially helpful in working through blockages. My clients often report profound shifts in their lives.

Working with clients, I've become aware of the need for a book that clearly and effectively teaches the basic concepts of Chinese medicine. I decided to write that book myself. The study and practice of Chinese medicine have been an extraordinary path of learning and growth for me. I hope this book will inspire the flame of awareness in all who read it.

Part I

Theories and Concepts

Chapter 1

Why Take This Trip?

THE ANCIENTS TAUGHT that every year is just a chapter in the book of life. Each of these chapters has its own beginning, middle, and end, with the four seasons making up a single year or cycle. The cycle begins with the spring, as the energy current of life is (re)born and we experience it rising and opening up. During the summer, the energy reaches its peak and we experience a natural sense of enhanced vitality. In autumn, as the leaves fall, the energy begins its decline. In the final stage, winter, the energy recedes until it finally passes away. This story repeats itself every 365 days or so, the time our planet takes to complete one trip around the sun. These cycles, visible in the largest celestial events as well as in the smallest microscopic processes, are the essence of life.

Humans share an inborn drive to live the best life possible. We continually strive to improve the quality of our emotional and physical life. In addition, each of us has a deeply rooted desire to connect to something larger than ourselves, some form of spiritual being. Achieving a state of well-being depends on developing a healthy body, clear mind, and vibrant spirit. The central thesis of this book is that we can do this most effectively when we are in harmony with the cycles of nature.

In the twentieth and twenty-first centuries, industrialization has made it ever harder for us to live in harmony with nature. When we were farmers and lived closer to the land, knowledge of the seasons was an essential survival skill; today's explosion of technology has pushed us away from a lifestyle that is intuitively natural. For all its benefits, technology has left many of us feeling lost and disconnected.

As we in the West have become familiar with Eastern philosophy, we've found a new vision of integrated health. We can create for ourselves a new state of wellness by studying the wisdom of the ancient Chinese masters, who excelled in applying the principals of living in harmony with natural cycles. These wise teachers stressed the importance of modifying our diets, herbal supplements, exercise, and meditation routines to match the changing seasons. By making changes in accordance with the changing energy of the seasons, we can achieve a level of health and well-being far beyond what we've experienced before.

Medicine in the Age of Technology

In recent generations, medicine has become increasingly technological. Advanced imaging equipment such as CAT scans and MRIs offer today's doctors sophisticated tools for diagnosing disease. Advanced surgeries and synthetic drugs are the treatments of choice, and they often provide what look like miracle cures. One big problem with this Western medical model is that its focus is only on curing diseases and preventing death — it neglects the promotion of health. This style of medicine has clear benefits, of course, but it must be seen in a larger perspective. Although Western medicine shines in the arena of trauma and in life-and-death situations, its usefulness in treating chronic illness and pain and in building health is limited, at best. "Alternative medicine," as it has been dubbed, focuses instead on increasing health

9

and quality of life. The special gift of traditional Chinese medicine is its understanding of how we can build our own state of vitality. The aim of this book is to help readers reclaim their power over their own health and vitality.

Chinese Philosophy and Medicine

The Chinese culture dates some 5,000 years and is closely intertwined with scientific observation. From their close observations of nature, the ancient Chinese masters learned the language of the cycles. And from this wealth of knowledge, the great theories and understandings of Chinese philosophy emerged. The most fundamental concept of this philosophy is that of *yin and yang*. This concept says that the universe can be seen as two opposing yet interconnected forces that are constantly moving and dancing with one another. Yin is defined as the dark, cool, and receptive portion of the cycle; yang is the light, warm, and active portion. The attempt to harmonize these two forces is at the heart of all Chinese theories.

As Chinese culture evolved, its philosophy gave birth to varied applications, including martial arts, meditation, medicine, writing and poetry, painting, music, and geomancy. All these forms share the same core philosophy.

Chinese medicine seeks to bring balance, harmony, and well-being to the individual. It looks at a person as a whole unit containing many different integrated systems. Through strengthening what is deficient and dispersing what is excessive, it seeks to optimize the whole person. This sounds simple, and it is. But this fundamental simplicity does not mean that the system lacks complexity, only that everything in it follows the natural order.

Learning to Flow with the Season

Seasonal energy offers a vast and powerful resource we can draw upon. It flows in large, sweeping movements and can be seen all around us — as the leaves change color, the days lengthen or shorten, and the spring bloom awakens. It is the energy current of the planet Earth: a slow and gentle process, one that we can't hurry along or change but that permeates each of our lives. Harmony with natural movements gives us a feeling of trust, an intuitive sense that helps in our decision making, our conflict resolution, and our self-knowledge. Although we can arrive at this state of being with relative ease, it requires discipline to maintain. Connecting with the seasonal cycles naturally brings about a healthier body, a clearer mind, and a more harmonious psyche and spirit.

This seasonal connection is available to all of us when we listen intently to nature and to ourselves. Nobody is excluded. It is free to all and the birthright of humankind. The benefits, however, take varying amounts of time, depending on how far out of rhythm we have strayed. No one can recover from a life of self-destructive excess overnight. Nature is powerful, but we must put in the time and effort.

In order to return our lives to balance, we must make changes in our lifestyle. You can begin this process by following the instructions in this book on diet, herbal therapy, exercise, chi kung, and meditation. Once you come to understand the underlying themes and meanings of the energy you're working with, you'll find it much easier to discover tools and techniques that work for you. The tools given in this book are powerful and effective, but they are not the only ones. In fact, the most powerful tools often are those you find on your own. I urge you to use the tools described in this book. Test them in your own life. See what works and what doesn't, find out why, and you'll begin to understand the essence of what you are doing; this will help you avoid the old pitfalls the next time you encounter them.

But what about people who live in areas where seasonal variations are small? While the seasons may not appear to change, the Earth still orbits the sun, and there is a difference in cosmic energy based on the Earth's position in its orbit. So, even though the leaves may not change color and snow may not fall, you can still observe

11

the atmospheric fluctuations that seasonal harmony is built upon. Even in the tropics, you'll find it enriching to alter aspects of your lifestyle in harmony with the changing cosmic energy.

The information in this book will familiarize you with the changing seasons, but the information and tools are merely guidelines. For instance, during the summer it's optimal to work out close to noon. But many people work during the day, of course, and it's impractical for them to work out at that time. Despite these limitations, it helps just to be aware of the energy that is manifested during the summer. Don't get caught up in the tools; learn from them, and use your knowledge to live a more harmonious life.

Chapter 2

Yin, Yang, and the Building Blocks of Chinese Alchemy

IN THE WEST, we think of ourselves as living in a molecular world. When we get sick, we believe our illness has been caused because a certain microbe has entered our system and our immune response has not been up to the task of resisting it. We believe our food is made up of molecules of potassium, calcium, magnesium, and so forth, and that the benefits we derive from it are based on the vitamins it contains. We understand the world based on a scientific view of energy.

The Chinese philosophic model also understands the world energetically, although the energy is more poetic than scientific. From this point of view, objects are in states of continual flux, always transforming from one state to another. What's important is the quality and quantity of energy something possesses. In the Eastern mindset, a person becomes sick because there is an imbalance in his or her vital energy. That imbalance might be caused by several factors. To treat the illness, a doctor needs to observe the signs and symptoms a patient exhibits and then rebalance the person's energy.

This energetic awareness is based on thousands of years of observation. As Chinese culture evolved, wise men and women developed terminology and theories to understand and classify what they saw. We will use these fundamental theories as we delve into the concepts of seasonal harmony and come to understand the world in energetic terms.

Yin and Yang

The concept of yin and yang, some 3,000 to 5,000 years old, is fundamental to Chinese philosophy and culture. Exactly how the words were coined is unclear, but there is some evidence that the concepts were an early part of Chinese philosophic evolution. Literally translated as "shady side of the hill" and "sunny side of the hill," yin and yang provide a basic model for viewing the universe. This fundamental contrast can be used to classify all aspects of the natural world.

Yin and yang are the two central characters in the dance of life — the polar opposites of one integrated system. They are totally dependent on one another; neither could exist without the other. They are constantly in motion and take turns leading and following. Neither is more powerful than the other; instead, their relationship involves a balance of power that is continually shifting.

Yin and yang eloquently describe the dynamic forces of the universe. Night and day, water and fire, female and male are just a few of the oppositional forces of nature that are both dependent on and defined by one another. One of the beautiful aspects of yin/yang theory is that it can be applied equally to the movement of heavenly bodies and to events in the human body. From the planets orbiting the sun to the respiration and heartbeat of the body, all things connect when seen through the lens of yin/yang theory.

Although yin and yang are defined by each other, it is still possible —even essential — to understand them individually. It is important to understand that neither is quantitatively or qualitatively "better." They are equal but opposite.

The force of yin is considered as female or receptive, the substance from which all things are created. It is the aspect of energy that is dark, cold, still, tranquil, and nourishing to life. In the energy cycle, it is where energy is gathered and stored to be used at another time.

Yang is seen as male or active, the aspect of energy that is light, moving, activating, and functional. It is the portion of the cycle when energy is used or burned. Because of its active and aggressive nature, yang often is seen more directly. But we shouldn't underestimate the importance of yin: It's yin that fuels all of yang's activities. There is no yang without yin, and vice versa.

Yin and yang are always viewed in relation to each other. Something that seems dark and cold can still be considered yang when compared to a substance that is darker and colder. It is important to view each object relative to what it is being compared to. When compared to one another, any two things can be seen as yin or yang. A common misconception in the West is that men are yang and women are yin. But many women are more active and aggressive then men and so can be seen as more yang. And many men are larger and have more mass then women and thus can be seen as more yin. It is important not to get caught up in the definitions. They are simply signs on the road — not the road itself.

Yin and yang are not just abstract concepts, they are real-world tools, and we can apply them to almost all aspects of life. They are symbols of rest and activity we can use on any scale, from microscopically to cosmically. We can see them in atoms and in the expansion and contraction of the universe. We can see them in cycles of seconds, minutes, hours, days, weeks, months, years, millennia.

No matter how strongly yin or yang something is, it always contains a little bit of the other. That is the meaning of the little black or white circle in the larger shape. Nothing is ever completely black or white. However extreme something becomes, it always has the ability to achieve balance.

15

The Five Phases and the Four Seasons

The yin/yang theory is both sublime and essential. We can use it to describe and classify any aspect of the natural world. However, sometimes we must define the cycles in more specific terms. By observing the seasons, the ancient Chinese masters refined the theory of yin/yang to create the *five phases*. The theory of the five phases breaks yin and yang each into two halves. Yin is seen as rising yin and full yin. Yang is seen as rising yang and full yang. The fifth phase is the state of balance that mediates between the expanded forms of yin and yang.

The Chinese masters gave names to each portion of this cycle. They called the rising yang (spring, in the yearly cycle) wood, the full yang (summer) fire, the rising yin (autumn) metal, and the full yin (winter) water. They realized that, even though the cycles were constantly in motion, there was a force that constantly maintained equilibrium. They called this great balancing force the *earth phase*. Earth is attributed to the late or Indian summer. The balancing energy of the earth phase is present any time a cycle is changing. So, here are the five phases:

- *Wood* burns to make fire.

- *Fire* burns to produce earth.

- *Earth* produces metal.

- *Metal* enriches the water.

- *Water* feeds the wood.

Within the five-phases is a theory that each element contains within itself all the other elements. This idea — that each part contains the pattern of the whole — is fundamental to Chinese philosophy. Macrocosm and microcosm both follow the same universal patterns.

The Eight Principles

Because yin/yang philosophy is the foundation of traditional Chinese thought, many other theories derive from it. The concept of the *eight principles* is one of these extensions. This theory describes a person or thing according to its relative yin or yang nature using four different determinations: *location*, interior (yin) or exterior (yang); *temperature*, cold (yin) or hot (yang); *amount of energy*, deficient (yin) or excessive (yang); and, finally, yin and yang themselves. Using these basic principles, we can see people more clearly in terms of their energetic nature.

Location helps us understand where the predominate energy lies. A person who is introspective, quiet, and withdrawn is considered an interior type of personality, whereas one who is extroverted, loud, and social is considered an exterior type of person.

Temperature is a way of classifying metabolic activity. A person who has cold hands and feet, likes to dress warmly, and prefers to be indoors is considered a cold

17

personality. Someone who is usually hot, does not like to wear many clothes, and enjoys being outside is understood as a hot personality.

The amount of energy a person has is a gauge of his or her overall state of being. Someone who has slow speech and pulses, is small, and tends to eat little is considered a deficient type of personality. A person who has fast speech and pulses, is large, and likes to eat a lot is considered an excess type of personality.

Keep in mind that these are just guidelines. Yin and yang themselves are understood only in terms of relativity. The eight principles are meant to be used in comparing one thing to another.

The Tao

As Imperial China evolved, some people became dissatisfied with society's corruption and went into the mountains to live in seclusion. As time passed, these people developed many spiritual systems, including Taoism. *The Tao* translates as "the way," and Taoism is the study and practice of finding and harmonizing with the way. "The Tao that can be spoken of is not the true Tao," wrote Lao Tzu, the founder of Taoism. The Tao might be compared to what we in the West think of as God. It is the infinite energy that permeates the universe.

The ultimate goal of Taoist practice is to reach a state of being known as *immortality*. The first step is cultivating good physical health and abundant energy reserves. The energy that is built is used to refine the spirit; with enough practice, the spirit can be elevated to a state of communion with the Tao. The process of transforming raw physical energy into heightened spiritual energy is called *alchemy*. The intention of Taoist practice is to build a state of good health so the practitioner can live long enough to achieve a state of bonding with the Tao. Immortality, according to Taoist thought, is the realization of that goal.

The Three Treasures

The *three treasures system* is an ancient form of Taoist alchemy. It is an effective tool for understanding and working with some of the basic forms of energy in the Chinese model. The concept was created by the Taoists to classify the different energies at work in the body during the alchemical process. These are called treasures because each energy is seen in its essential, purest, most precious form. The energies are *jing*, which means vital essence; *chi*, vital energy; and *shen*, spirit. The three treasures system is one of the oldest and most profound forms of alchemy. The basic premise is that jing creates chi, chi creates shen, shen creates chi, and chi creates jing. In this cycle, the whole is enhanced by working on three different aspects of the being. A simple metaphor for describing the treasures is the candle. The wax of the candle is the jing. The flame is the chi. The light the candle gives off is the shen.

Jing

Jing is the densest and coarsest treasure in the body. Jing is considered the fundamental energy of life, and it literally permeates every physical structure of the body. Jing often is called the root of life. In Western terms it might be thought of as the body's genes or genetic potential. The quantity and quality of our jing plays an important role in our potential life span and our overall vitality. Jing is said to be the energy we receive from our parents at the time of our conception; therefore, according to Chinese philosophy, jing can be traced back to the beginning of life. Jing also is closely related to what the Chinese call the *ming men*. This is the primal flame that powers all metabolic activity in the body. In order for ming men to burn, a small portion of our jing is required for every physiologic transformation in the body. It is the reserve energy we need to adapt to all the stresses in our life.

According to traditional Chinese medicine (TCM), jing is stored in the body's kidney system. This system presides over the physical structure of the body. It in-

19

cludes the reproductive fluids, functions, organs, the ears and the auditory system, the bones and teeth, the brain, the adrenal glands, and the endocrine system. Jing rules the processes of reproduction. It also fuels the body's healing and repair functions. Although shen presides over the intellectual, emotional, and spiritual aspect of the mind — preventing it from becoming muddled by anxiety or excessive emotionalism—jing rules the mind's power and inherited potential. Strong jing produces a sharp, keen mind that's able to learn and grow. Jing is intimately connected with the endocrine system and the various hormones. Abundant jing ensures that our hormones will be plentiful and balanced, whereas a deficiency of jing may result in hormonal imbalances or malfunction.

It is essential to protect our jing. Life naturally consumes jing, and a lifestyle of excessive smoking, drinking, drug use, over-exercising, over-working, and too much play burns jing at an even faster rate. Excessive sexual behavior will drain jing especially quickly. Men lose a small amount of jing every time they ejaculate, and women lose a significant amount during childbirth. Consistent and prolonged stress also leads to a loss of jing. Jing is consumed when we are pushed past the limits of fatigue to exhaustion. The body then is depleted of the energy it needs to recover from exertion and is forced to consume a portion of the jing stored deep inside. We are born with a finite amount of jing; when it runs, out we die. Although it is extremely difficult to replace jing and fairly easy to consume it, with a proper diet, herbs, exercise, meditation, and other practices we can protect and strengthen it. I'll be discussing some of these techniques in the section on the water element (winter).

Strengthening jing can lead to an overall increase in our body's health and vitality. It also invigorates the lower back, the knees, the ankles, the power of thought, our creative energy, our sexual energy, and our ability to adapt to stress.

20

Chi

Chi, second treasure, is roughly translated as air, breath, or vital energy. It's a concept that describes energy and its many functions and permutations. Chi can be used not only to describe certain functions within the body but also to describe a characteristic of something. "The house has good chi" is a way of saying that the house makes you feel good, that there is something positive or soothing about it. In terms of bodily functions, chi refers to the vital energy of metabolism and emotion. Closely related to the power of digestion and respiration, chi is our quantity of daily energy. It's also the quality of our energy. Chi is not a static force that can be bottled and put in storage — it needs to flow. It is a current of energy that flows through pathways called *meridians* (which I will discuss in the next section). Its strength is measured, in part, by how well it moves.

Chi is the energy we make, use, and consume on a daily basis. We derive this energy from our food and from the air we breathe. When these two energy sources are combined, they form chi. Chi is involved in all of the metabolic activities of our body. The basic energy we have on a daily basis is derived from how much chi we have and how well it is flowing. Chi has many functions within the body. It governs a part of our immune system and helps to determine our emotional life. If chi flows smoothly, the body and mind are harmonious and tranquil. If it becomes stuck or blocked in certain areas, pain and disease ensue. According to Eastern medicine, one of the essential definitions of disease is a blockage of chi flow.

According to TCM, chi and blood work together to circulate fresh energy through the body while removing used energy. Blood, which is considered yin relative to chi, is formed by adding a small portion of jing to chi. Chi is the activating force that gives the blood its movement. If either our chi or our blood is deficient or stagnant, we will experience disease and pain. The quality and quantity of our chi and our blood, as well as how well they flow, constitute a major factor in our overall health.

21

Shen

Shen is perhaps the most precious of all the treasures, because it is our higher awareness. The word *shen* also means spirit, soul, or consciousness. Shen is what separates humans from animals: It is our ability to rise above the illusion of the physical, dualistic world and see into the world of the divine. It is the energy of awareness and compassion and is responsible for our spiritual outlook and our mental and psychological well-being.

Shen is said to be stored in the heart, and it has an intimate relationship with the emotions and all functions of the heart. Shen is not the heart itself, but a subtle energy linked to our divine nature. Associated with love, joy, kindness, charity, prayer, and spirituality, shen is the knowledge that all things are one.

Cultivating the Treasures

Each of the three treasures relies on the other two to complete and sustain itself. When one treasure is tonified or purified, it adds to the well-being of the whole system. On the other hand, when one treasure is out of balance or becomes depleted, the whole system goes out of balance. Later, we'll look at how diet, herbs, exercise, chi kung, and meditation in combination with seasonal harmony can balance and develop all three treasures.

The Asian Perspective on Organs and Internal Connections

As the ancient masters observed nature both externally and internally, they learned of the deep integration of all things. They realized that, as the seasons changed, a different energy was awakened within the body, and they saw that this energy contained many different factors. Each season stimulated one organ most directly, and each organ had a distinctive emotional spectrum associated with it. Thus the ancient masters understood that an organ is more than a single object within the body — rather, it is a compilation of systems, functions, fluids, and emotions. It is, in fact, a network of functions that combine to form an organ system. They also realized that all of the organs and their functions were linked together. If one organ functioned too strongly or not strongly enough, the others would be impaired.

The ancients described each organ as having an energy pathway or meridian associated with it. The meridian can be understood as a river or network of energy that carries chi and blood throughout the body. The course the meridians take through the body is not haphazard. The energy pathways are specific and move with precision according to our mood, our environment, the time of day, the time of year, our age, and our general health.

In the Asian paradigm there are twelve recognized organ systems, each with an associated meridian. Six of the organs are considered to be yin, and six are seen as yang. Yin organs in general are solid, whereas yang organs are hollow. Each yin organ is paired with a yang organ of similar function, but the yin organs are seen as more important. The pairings are these:

Yin	Yang
Liver	Gall bladder
Heart	Small intestine
Spleen	Stomach
Lungs	Large intestine
Kidneys	Bladder
Pericardium	San jiao (meaning triple burner)

The last two organs have supportive roles to the heart (pericardium) and the kidneys (san jiao). I will discuss the characteristics of each of the organs and their functions in following chapters.

23

Although the yang organs and their functions are important, I will focus more on the yin organs. In general, the yang organs have similar and complementary functions to their yin counterparts.

Each organ system is also ruled by a certain part of the day. As chi flows through the body, it gathers most intensively in one organ system and meridian for two hours of the day. This awareness gave rise to the *meridian clock*.

Organ	Time of the Day
Lungs	3 A.M. – 5 A.M.
Large intestine	5 A.M. – 7 A.M.
Stomach	7 A.M. – 9 A.M.
Spleen	9 A.M. – 11 A.M.
Heart	11 A.M. – 1 P.M.
Small intestine	1 P.M. – 3 P.M.
Bladder	3 P.M. – 5 P.M.
Kidneys	5 P.M. – 7 P.M.
Pericardium	7 P.M. – 9 P.M.
San jiao	9 P.M. – 11 P.M.
Gall bladder	11 P.M. – 1 A.M.
Liver	1 A.M. – 3A.M.

In TCM, one learns to evaluate each of the organ energy systems according to its overall function, just as if each has a gas gauge. Once we are trained how to look, we can read it. If an organ system is doing its duties effectively, without struggle, we say it is functioning well. If it is accomplishing its tasks too quickly and disrupting the functions of other organs, we say it is excessive and needs to have some energy shifted away from it. If an organ system is not accomplishing its tasks, we say it is deficient or dysfunctional. In this case, the organ either needs more energy shifted to it or its underlying dysfunction repaired.

Each organ system in the body has a preferred state of being and is harmed by certain pathologies. According to TCM, these include wind, cold (on a spectrum to extreme cold), heat (on a spectrum to pathological fire, which should not be confused with the *element* of fire), dampness (on a spectrum to phlegm), dryness, and summer heat. The pathologies are climatic forces that have penetrated the body in excessive amounts so the body's natural functions are disrupted.

According to TCM, it's less important to determine the cause of disease and more important to observe the patterns and relationships within the disharmony. Therefore, TCM practitioners commonly treat the signs and symptoms a patient presents and are not as concerned with pathogenesis. Thus, TCM does not offer elaborate theories of the causative factors of disease. Rather, it has developed observational techniques for diagnosis and treatment of disease. Practitioners also consider the factors that put the body into a state that allows pathological energy to enter. So they do an evaluation of a patient's lifestyle — including diet, exercise, stress levels, sexual habits, the home environment, emotional and psychological states, and spiritual outlook — to help them understand the underlying cause of the disease. Although the treatment of disease is important and necessary, it is seen as a lesser form of medicine. The true art of TCM is in the building of profound states of wellness.

The Basic Pathologies

When considering the pathologies, it's generally best to describe the symptoms typically associated with them. According to TCM, we must understand how these pathologies manifest in the body and what treatments can be applied to remove them. The superior doctor, however, is one who can keep his patients healthy by perceiving disease before it presents itself. In fact, in ancient China, a doctor was paid only when a patient was well. If the patient became ill, the doctor had not done a good job.

Certain pathologies typically affect the body more in certain seasons. For instance, cold affects the body in winter. Although these seasonal associations are accurate and valuable, they are only guidelines. We can contract any of the pathologies at any time of year, especially if there is an underlying disharmony within the body. For example, a person can acquire a heat invasion in the winter if she is deficient in yin or has some other form of disharmony with her heating and cooling mechanisms.

Wind

Wind is a force that produces movement in what would otherwise be still. According to TCM, the body is most susceptible to wind during the spring. Wind rarely presents alone and often serves a vehicle for other pathologies to gain entrance to the body. Wind is a yang pathology; it affects the superficial, upper, and outer portions of the body. Wind disorders affect the lungs, skin, face, and muscles. Symptoms of a wind invasion are rapid-onset fever and chills, skin eruptions, pain that moves from place to place, tremors, spasms, convulsions, and dizziness. When discussing wind it is important to distinguish between *exterior* and *interior* wind. Exterior wind is most often accompanied by other pathological energies, such as cold, heat, or damp. In the West, we often think of exterior wind pathologies as contagious illnesses such as a cold or flu virus. The hallmark symptoms are fever and chills, cough, sore throat, congested sinuses, headache, body aches, skin eruptions, and

26

aversion to drafts. Internal wind is more complicated and is connected to chronic and elaborate patterns of disharmony. It typically involves both the liver and some form of deep-seated disharmony. Symptoms consist of spasms, skin eruptions, tremors, dizziness, and tinnitus. In more severe cases, internal wind can manifest as what we in the West term a stroke.

When wind combines with another pathology, the signs and symptoms will be a blend of both. For example, if cold is attached to the wind (forming a wind–cold invasion), we will see wind symptoms mixed with symptoms of the cold pathology (which we'll discuss in the next section). To treat external wind invasion, we must open the pores, induce sweat, and push the wind out of the body. This is known as *diaphoresis*. Internal wind is treated by removing the wind from the body while addressing the underlying disharmony that allowed the wind to manifest. This usually involves harmonizing the liver, removing stagnation, and nourishing the yin and blood.

Cold

Cold is a yin pathology — a force that cools and contracts. According to TCM, the body is most affected by cold during winter. The defining symptoms of cold are a feeling of chill somewhere in the body and an aversion to cold. In general, cold takes time to set in, but once it does, it is difficult to release because it tends to affect the lower, internal, and deep portions of the body. Cold causes things to contract and slow, often obstructing the normal flow of chi and blood. This causes stiffness and pain and impairs normal physiologic activities and functions.

It is important to differentiate between *exterior* cold and *interior* cold. External cold often enters the body with wind, causing the body to be cold, have an aversion to cold, produce a lot of clear sinus secretions, and have headaches and body aches. The body also can exhibit strong chills with a mild fever.

The internal cold pathology often is related to a deficiency of yang, and it takes time to develop. As it does it impairs the digestive fire and overall metabolic activity of the body, causing slowness. One of the main symptoms of internal cold is pain — especially pain affecting the knees, lower back, and joints. If internal cold lingers long enough, it ultimately harms the *yang jing*, or active form of deep life force. Usually, a prior underlying weakness in the yang jing already exists. This preexisting weakness allows the cold to penetrate in the first place.

External cold is treated with warming techniques that cause the pores to open and the body to sweat. It is important to address external cold invasion before it has time to settle in and lodge itself in the body. If external cold is allowed to set in, it can lead to internal cold. Interior cold is treated with techniques that warm the yang jing at its deepest level. People with a deficiency of yang may spend many years restoring their deep primal fire.

Heat and Fire

Heat is a force that produces "reckless" movement. This movement is seen in the blood, the mind, and the shen. According to TCM, the body is most susceptible to heat during the summer. Heat is a yang pathology, affecting the superficial, upper, and outer portions of the body. When affected by this force, the body feels hot and its functions become hyperactive. The face often becomes red, a high fever might be seen, and the urine can become dark with a significant reduction in volume. There may be bleeding, especially from the nose and gums. The body's fluids become depleted and often look yellowish upon excretion.

The pathological state of fire is at one end of the heat spectrum. This should not be confused with the *element* of fire, or with the normal fire within the body. In its extreme state, pathological fire can produce various forms of inflammation, ulcers, mania, extreme confusion, delirium, spontaneous bleeding, fainting, high fevers with extreme sweating, burning diarrhea, and explosive vomiting.

External heat usually combines with wind to enter the body. Symptoms include high fever with mild or no chills, sweating, aversion to heat, desire for cold things, dryness, thirst, headaches, sore throat, yellow sinus and lung excretions, irritability, and disturbed sleep patterns.

The heart, stomach, lungs, large intestine, and kidneys are affected by internal heat, which is most commonly found in those who have a preexisting condition of yin or fluid deficiency. Because of this deficiency, there is not enough coolness and moisture in the body to keep the yang in balance. Internal heat is characterized by hyperactivity, irritability, redness, a feeling of being hot, mild to strong fever, thirst, constipation, scanty dark urine, dark, thick bodily secretions, mania, delirium, and difficulty sleeping. The main difference between external and internal heat is that internal heat is more severe.

External heat is treated by expelling the heat while replenishing yin and moisture. As with other external pathologies, it is important to expel the heat before it has time to lodge itself in the body. If it is allowed to lodge itself, there will be a steady consumption of yin and body fluids until the patient has an imbalance of yin and yang. Internal heat is treated by cooling, moisturizing, and replenishing the body. Often it's necessary to use somewhat drastic measures to "put out the fire" within the body. It's also important to harmonize the heart, stomach, lungs, large intestine, and kidneys while healing from a condition of internal heat.

Summer Heat

Summer heat, a yang pathology, is a continuation of heat pathology. It is a purely external pathogen that results from excessive exposure to hot summer weather. Symptoms include being overheated, sudden high fever with profuse sweating, dehydration, fainting, and delirium.

29

Summer heat pathology is treated by removing the person from the sun, cooling the body, and replenishing lost fluids. The patient should lie down to avoid fainting. Summer heat is synonymous with what we sometimes call sunstroke or heat stroke.

Dampness

Dampness — or, in its extreme state, phlegm — is a yin pathology that is heavy, turbid, and lingering. According to TCM, the body is most affected by dampness during the Indian or late summer (the earth element). Dampness affects digestive processes most directly. When the body's digestive fire or primal fire (yang jing) are weak, it is more susceptible to damp invasion. The defining symptoms of dampness are heaviness, slowness, and excessive turbid secretions. These include thick diarrhea, heavy vaginal discharge, and oozing skin eruptions. Patients commonly feel a sense of fullness and of being soggy and water-logged. Dampness tends to affect the lower portions of the body, as it is heavy and thus sinks. It often obstructs the normal physiologic functions as it slows down, congeals, and inhibits the circulation of energy.

External and internal dampness are similar, distinguishable only by location and onset. External dampness tends to enter the body with wind and is found in the external aspects, such as the skin. It usually is resolved fairly quickly. Internal dampness develops because of an underlying deficiency and is found deeper within the body. Internal dampness tends to take a long time to resolve. When the body is cold and yang-deficient, there is a greater chance for dampness to set in.

The treatment of dampness involves methods that warm and transform the damp energy. At the same time it is important to expel cold, strengthen kidney energy, and warm the digestive yang. Dampness is one of the most difficult pathogens to treat, as it is slow moving and lingering by nature. In its later stages it is called *phlegm*. Phlegm is dampness that has had time to congeal and harden. It often forms an exterior membranous layer that makes it difficult to contend with. From a Western point of view, candida, obesity, cysts, lipomas, and cancerous tumors are forms of dampness and phlegm.

Dryness

Dryness happens when there is not enough moisture and fluid to nourish the body. According to TCM, the body is most affected by dryness in the autumn. Dryness affects the respiratory system most directly, because the lungs require moisture to function well. Dryness is an external pathogen that usually enters the body with wind. It tends to manifest in those who have an underlying yin deficiency. It also is found in the body after a period of excess heat, stress, or lack of sleep. Symptoms include a dry, hacking cough, dry sinuses, wheezing, chest pain, slight lingering fevers, nose bleeds, and dry eyes. Dryness also produces an internal environment where other yin-deficiency symptoms can develop.

External and internal dryness are similar, differing only in the way they develop. External dryness often presents after a period of hot, dry, and windy weather. This type of weather, commonly found in the desert, can dry out the body and especially the lungs. Internal dryness usually develops in patients with long-standing excesses of heat. The excess heat slowly but consistently consumes yin and moisture until there are rampant dry and yin-deficiency symptoms.

The treatment of dryness involves removing the excess heat, cooling the body, and replenishing the moisture that has been consumed. If dryness is detected early, it is relatively easy to treat.

Stagnation

Stagnation is not classically considered a pathology in and of itself. It is, however, an important concept that affects most people today. Within TCM, disease and pain are defined by blockages of energy. Stagnation develops from too much sitting, too

31

much television, too much meat, and too much stress, or from the consumption of or exposure to harmful chemicals or drugs. Stagnation develops from an unhealthy lifestyle. It affects the entire body and especially the liver. General symptoms are imbalanced emotions, including depression, anger, rage, and feelings of being disconnected. Stagnation also manifests as various pains, including headaches, body aches, and sore muscles. It can also play a role in various immune system breakdowns, including recurrent colds and flu. Stagnation tends to exacerbate other disharmonies in the body.

The treatment of stagnation involves adopting a more balanced lifestyle, eating less meat, watching less television, getting more exercise and fresh air, and taking steps to balance stress levels and the emotions.

These are the basic pathologies as defined in TCM. While each organ system is adversely affected by many of the same unhealthy lifestyle patterns and pathologies, some behaviors and pathogens affect certain organs more specifically. Table 1 (see p. 30) shows which pathologies affect which organs, and what state each organ prefers.

Each of the organ systems also has an emotional spectrum, with a positive and a negative emotional pole. Within TCM and Chinese philosophy there is no separation of mind and body. All of the various processes and functions happen together and affect one another. If a particular emotion becomes unbalanced, it affects a corresponding organ. If a particular organ becomes unbalanced, it has an adverse effect on an associated emotion. When an organ is functioning well, it emits positive aspects of emotion; when it is functioning poorly, it emits negative forms of emotion. When we experience a certain emotion, it affects an associated organ —for example, positive emotions help our organs to function better, and negative emotions weaken our organs. In each seasonal chapter, I will discuss which organs are associated with particular emotions and how they affect one another.

Organ system	Preferred state	Behaviors causing problems	Pathologies
Liver	Cool, calm, and smooth, with an abundance of liver yin and blood	Excessive anger, alcohol, drugs, and smoking	Stagnation, heat, dryness, internal wind, and deficiency of yin and blood
Heart and pericardium	Cool, with an abundance of heart yin and blood	Lack of sleep and excessive emotionalism	Heat, stagnation, and deficiency of yin and blood
Spleen	Warm and dry	Consumption of fried foods, excessive cold and damp, excessive spicy food	Dampness, cold, and summer heat
Lungs	Cool and moist	Smoking and breathing polluted air	Dryness, heat, cold, and external wind
Kidneys	Warm, with an abundance of yin and yang	Excessive sexuality and childbirth	Excessive heat or cold, dampness, deficiency of yin or yang

Table 1

Basic Terms

Throughout this book you will find statements such as, "The liver is in charge of the smooth flow of chi," or "The lungs control the skin." These functional associations evolved from centuries of observation. As you begin your study of TCM, it is important not to get bogged down trying to understand *why* specific attributes are connected with particular organs. It's better simply to accept these connections until you have a working understanding of the medicine and philosophy.

Another concept you'll see is the combination of organ systems and types of energy, such as "liver chi" or "heart yin." Often, it's necessary to discuss the functionality of a certain organ system, and "liver chi," for example, is a way of picturing the functionality of the liver energy system. In the same way, "heart yin" is a way of describing the relative amount of yin in the heart's functional capacity.

Chapter 3

Tools of the Trade

Tools

For centuries, diet, herbal therapy, exercise, chi kung, introspection, and meditation have been keys to harmonizing with nature and restoring balance in life. These techniques have stood the test of time on their own merits. When we understand how to modify aspects of our lives and adapt them to the flow of nature, we move directly toward our goal of balance, well-being, and seasonal harmony.

Diet

 The most fundamental tool available to us is diet. What we eat has a direct effect on our health and emotional outlook. Flavors, temperatures, and colors are among the factors that influence the way food affects us. The old saying "You are what you eat" is true. It is important to eat foods that are whole, natural, and organic and that contain as few artificial ingredients as possible.

Using diet to be in harmony with the seasons follows a clear pattern. In the springtime, when the seasonal energy rises and opens, it is important to eat foods that are light and easy to digest, such as steamed vegetables, fruits, light soups, rice dishes, and fish. It's wise to cut down on heavy foods, such as meats, fried or fatty foods, oily foods, and desserts.

In the summer, when energy is at its peak and the weather is hot, it's important to eat foods that support the fullness of our energy. The summer diet is similar to the spring diet, although during summer it is especially important to consume fluids.

In the autumn, as energy begins to decline and move inward, it's time to begin eating foods that are more substantial and that have been cooked longer. Soups and thick stews work well to add substance and warmth. During the autumn it's also wise to include more meat in your diet, because it is a substantial food source. Many people don't eat meat for moral, ethical, or spiritual reasons, but it is important to recognize that eating good-quality meat in small quantities builds health and well-being. While I do not want to undermine the vegetarian philosophy, there are time-appropriate benefits of consuming meat. The autumn diet prepares us for the slumber of winter. This does not mean that eating unhealthy foods is acceptable. Rather, the goal is to eat a larger quantity of healthy foods.

During winter our energy is deep and slow, and in most parts of the world the weather is cold. It's crucial during this cold season to eat foods that are substantial and warming. The winter diet is similar to the autumn diet, except in winter there's more emphasis on warming foods. In chapters on the specific seasons, I will go into more detail about what foods to eat and how to prepare them.

As we explore the concept of modifying diet to harmonize with the seasons, note that the changes I recommend are gentle ones. Throughout the year it's important to eat a healthy, balanced diet. The basic foods recommended for any given season may even be the same. What changes are the way they are prepared and the amounts that are consumed.

In the West, our approach to diet generally is limited to the molecular content of food. Meat, for instance, contains so many grams of protein, so many grams of fat, and a total of so many calories. Another successful philosophy combines this molecular knowledge with the energetic understanding of food. *Food is energy.* This means that, in addition to having a certain nutritional content, any given food has an energetic "personality." TCM categorizes foods energetically by temperature, by what organs they stimulate, by what organs they weaken, and by other energetic actions.

In Chinese philosophy, *taste* is not just something to be appreciated; rather, it's another tool for understanding the world in energetic terms. Within the Chinese model there are five basic tastes, each associated with a phase or element — and, by extension, a season, an organ, an emotion, and so on. The five tastes are shown in Table 2.

Taste	Action	Balancing taste	Element	Organ	Season
Sour	Astringing	Pungent	Wood	Liver	Spring
Bitter	Cooling and dispersing	Salty	Fire	Heart	Summer
Sweet	Nourishing	Itself	Earth	Spleen	Late summer
Pungent	Activating	Sour	Metal	Lungs	Autumn
Salty	Consolidating	Bitter	Water	Kidneys	Winter

Table 2

Sweet and pungent tastes are thought of as yang. They have the properties of moving upward and outward and of warming and activating the body. Bitter, sour, and salty are yin. They have the properties of moving downward and inward and are cooling and sedating to the body. During the course of the year it's wise to eat foods that represent all these tastes. To achieve seasonal harmony, we should use the tastes as tools to enhance balance.

The *color* of food is another important tool. Not only does it reflect a food's energetic state, it inspires the eyes to make the meal stimulating on multiple levels. We need to eat foods of different colors. The color correspondences are shown in Table 3.

Color	Action	Balancing color	Element	Organ	Season
Green	Revitalizing	White	Wood	Liver	Spring
Red	Activating	Black or dark blue	Fire	Heart	Summer
Yellow	Nourishing	Itself	Earth	Spleen	Late summer
White or gray	Moisturizing	Green	Metal	Lungs	Autumn
Black or dark blue	Toning and rich	Red	Water	Kidneys	Winter

Table 3

Another important dietary tool is *preparation*. The way food is prepared affects the kind of energy it will provide. The longer food is cooked, the deeper and more substantial its energy becomes. The less food is cooked, the more superficial and dispersed the energy remains. The basic methods of cooking, from most superficial to most substantial, are steaming, sautéing, frying, broiling, grilling, boiling, and baking. In each seasonal chapter, I will discuss the diet that best supports that season, including tastes, colors, and appropriate cooking methods.

Dietary guidelines for each season apply to all meals; there's no real distinction between breakfast, lunch, and dinner. The same meals can be eaten at any time of the day. If your personal preference is to eat "traditional" breakfast foods for breakfast, for example, simply do so within the framework of the seasonal guides.

As you develop deeper connections to the seasons, your relationship with each of the energies will become clearer. At this point, diet can be especially effective for you. In the beginning, you might have to experiment to learn the effects of different foods. But if you simply listen to your body, it will give you valuable feedback.

Herbal Therapy

The next tool we have to work with is herbal therapy. This is beginning to gain popularity in the West as we become more aware of its benefits. In the modern era, we've moved so far from the soil and growing our own foods that most people are deficient in essential nutrients. Because of this, vitamin supplements have become especially important. To ensure proper nutrition, it's a good idea to take a wide-spectrum vitamin supplement. Herbs, however, serve a different purpose. We might think of them as super foods, or even as undomesticated vegetables. They give our bodies substances not found in most foods and can directly improve the quality of our energy. Herbs are rich in vitamins, minerals, and antioxidants, as well as many rare and highly beneficial substances. Or, as the Chinese would say, "Herbs build your chi." Consistently taking the right herbs will have a tremendous support on your general energy level; over time it will help you build a strong and balanced immune and endocrine system.

Throughout our evolution as a species, herbs have been an important part of our diet. Since the time we were hunters and gatherers, our diet has included roots, barks, leaves, and flowers from the natural world. It was only after humans transitioned to living in industrialized societies that our knowledge about herbs has been forgotten. With that loss we have broken our connection to nature and to natural cycles. Herbs are still available to us, however, and with the advancement of modern research, many of the benefits our ancestors knew are coming back into our consciousness.

39

Herbal therapy has been an important part of Chinese medicine's evolution. In fact, the world's first doctors were tribesmen who lived in the bush. For them, the knowledge of herbs was life-saving, and this knowledge was passed down from generation to generation. Until the time of Shen Nong, it was transmitted through an oral tradition. Shen Nong — the first Chinese emperor, who lived sometime before the second century C.E. — is credited with writing the *Shen-Nong Ben-Cao Jing* (*Pharmacopoeia Classic of the Divine Husbandman*). Although the original manuscript has been lost, there is a surviving text said to have been written many years later.

Shen Nong's *Pharmacopoeia* was the first book of its kind. It described a system of classifying herbs that is still in use today, recognizing 365 medicinal substances and arranging them in three classes. The highest grade is called the upper class of herbs (or the rulers), which are the most valuable due to their nonpoisonous, life-enhancing, longevity-promoting, and nutritional qualities. The *Pharmacopoeia* states that, if you want to prolong your life without aging, you should consume the herbs of the upper class. The middle grade of herbs is called the middle class (or the ministers). These are regulating and supportive herbs that are slightly harsh to the human body but not toxic. They are used to prevent illness and to balance deficiencies. The lowest grade, called the lower class of herbs (or the assistants), are considered medicinal in nature and used to rid the body of disease. The *Pharmacopoeia* says this class of herbs should be taken only for short periods of time, due to their toxic nature and the probability of harmful side effects.

Over thousands of years, much has been learned about Chinese herbs. Within the upper class are many herbs that have legendary effectiveness. Often called *tonics*, these herbs can be taken on a continual basis to promote good of body, mind, and spirit. They are not used to treat disease, but are prized for their ability to strengthen and support the body's innate healing powers. It was the discovery and use of these tonic herbs that created such a high standard for Chinese doctors. Ancient Chinese doctors were paid only as long as a patient was healthy; if the patient became sick, people believed the doctor was not doing his or her job. So, the doctor was not paid until the patient regained his or her health. This form of treatment was known as superior medicine — the strengthening and tonifying of the body to build a state of good health in which the body is able to regulate itself and remain free from disease.

The herbs and formulas I will discuss are predominately from the upper class, with a few middle-class herbs here and there. The lower-class herbs are beyond the scope of this book. Although these herbs are valuable and, if applied correctly, can help people to heal from serious diseases, their application should be overseen by a trained professional. The main purpose for using herbs in our context is to harmonize with the seasonal energy and build a profound state of integrated wellness. As I describe each season, I will offer some specific recommendations of appropriate herbs and formulas.

Consuming and Preparing Herbs

There are many ways to consume herbs. Due to its unique makeup, each herb has a method that's optimal. The basic ways to ingest herbs are either in some form of extract or by eating them directly. In most cases, an extract is the more powerful way of consuming herbs. Up to a certain point, the more concentrated the extract is, the more effective it will be. When you eat the whole herb, you ingest a lot of biomass along with the active ingredients. By extracting the active ingredients from the herb, you reduce the amount of biomass that must be digested and concentrate the amount of active ingredient that can be absorbed.

The are several ways to extract the beneficial qualities from herbs, as shown in Table 4.

41

Type of extraction	Method	Benefits
Water extraction	The herbs are brewed as a tea.	This is the most traditional way of extracting herbs and has been considered the best way to harmonize the actions of the herbs being cooked.
Infusion	Soak the herbs in hot water for 1 to 5 minutes.	This method is used to capture light, volatile aspects of herbs.
Tincturing	The herbs are soaked in alcohol for a prolonged period.	Also a traditional method of extracting herbs, the alcohol gives the extract an extra boost of warmth and invigoration.
Concentrated alcohol and water	These are made with specialized extraction equipment.	This is the best and easiest way to consume and assimilate herbs.
Spray-dried extraction	Herbs are brewed as tea in a concentrated form, then the extraction is spray-dried into a powder.	This is the best way to get concentrated extracts into capsules and powders.
Grinding into powder	Herbs are ground into a powder and the powder is pressed into tablets.	For most herbs, this is a waste, because the body has difficulty digesting the often dense and fibrous matter of the herbs.

Table 4

Generally, the more concentrated the extract the better. Herbs that are ground up and pressed into tablets are much less valuable; the more biomass the body has to digest, the less active ingredient it can absorb. Also, the process of digesting all of the biomass can harm the digestive system because of the enormous amount of energy it requires to do so. Many commercially available herb products are simply ground up herbs. Some of these products may be based on great formulas, but the products often are useless because the herbs either are not digestible or require too much time and energy to digest. Herbal products that go through a commercial form of extraction are much more valuable. Many commercial extractions produce highly concentrated extracts that are far more beneficial than powdered herbs.

The concentration of an herbal product is as expressed as a ratio. For example, 4:1, 8:1, or even a 1:1. The ratio describes the amount of herb, measured in pounds, that went into the extraction machine and the amount of extract, measured in gallons, that came out. In the case of a 4:1, four pounds of herbs were used to produce one gallon of extract.

When choosing herbs, keep in mind the saying, "Garbage in, garbage out." It's vital to get the highest-quality herbs available. Higher-quality herbs are more potent because they contain larger and more highly refined amounts of the active ingredients.

Of course, higher-quality herbs usually are more expensive. Here are a few guidelines for seeking out high-quality herbs.

- Often, *bigger is better*, although there are exceptions. It's best to have a large, well-formed herb. Avoid puny, underweight, shriveled-up herbs.

- *Age* is an important indicator of quality, especially for ginseng roots. The older the ginseng root, the more refined its active ingredients are. Older roots tend to be smaller and weigh less, but they are more potent.

- Another important gauge is *color*. Try to get herbs that have vibrant colors. If you're using an herb that's yellow, try to obtain herbs that are *vibrant* yellow. The vibrancy of the color usually is a good indicator of potency.

- Finally, it's essential to choose herbs that look and smell *fresh*. In fact, it's best if the herb looks as if it's just been picked and has a distinctive smell. If you settle for shriveled-up herbs that look decayed and decrepit, their effectiveness is likely to be similar.

43

When you're buying commercially extracted pills and liquids, gauging quality is more challenging, as you cannot see the herbs that went in to making them. Price can be a useful guideline here. Typically, the more expensive the product (within reason), the more potent and higher quality it is. If you get a bottle of herbs for five dollars, it's unlikely that the herbs are of high quality or will be effective. One of the most important tests is to see how a product makes you feel. If you can really see and feel the effects, then it's worth what you paid for it. If monetary considerations intervene, know that it's far better to take fewer high-quality herbs than to take more of a lower quality.

The most basic way to take herbs is to extract them in water by brewing them. This involves bringing the appropriate amount of water to a boil, turning it down to a simmer, and putting in the herbs. Cooking times vary: Generally, the lower on the plant the herb grows, the longer it needs to cook. Thus, roots and barks cook longest, whereas flowers and leaves need to cook for only a short time. Roots, barks, and other hard herbs might be cooked for up five hours, but the average cooking time for thick, hard herbs is about two hours. Cooking these herbs for long periods ensures that every bit of the active ingredients gets extracted. Leaves and flowers need simmer for just one to five minutes. These herbs are sensitive, and the active ingredients tend to be so light and volatile that they begin to evaporate after more then five minutes. When brewing a tea with both hard roots and sensitive flowers, you should first cook the hard herbs for a couple of hours, then add the light herbs for the last five minutes. Then remove the pot from the heat and drain off the liquid. Herbal teas brewed like this can be bottled, refrigerated, and safely consumed for up to a week.

Cooking herbs is an art form. You need to get to know the herbs you're using and allot enough time to extract their essence.

Some herbs contain ingredients that are not water-soluble; these must be extracted by alcohol soaking. In the West, we call this *tincturing*; in ancient China, it was called a *chiew*. The word literally translates as herbal wine. Alcohol extraction is a relatively easy process — you just soak the herbs in alcohol for at least six weeks. The higher the alcohol concentration, the faster the active ingredients will extract. With this method, all the herbs in a formula can be put into the container at the same time and left to soak indefinitely. In fact, many alcohol extractions taste and work better after years of soaking. Many herbs have both water- and alcohol-soluble ingredients and can be extracted into the medium that you prefer.

If you are new to herbs, start with a commercially extracted product made by a company you trust. That way you'll avoid having to buy and extract your own herbs. In most cases, commercial extracts are more effective than homemade remedies.

One of the most important aspects of an herbal program is consistent consumption. Usually, it's not necessary to take large quantities of herbs, as long as the herbs are consumed on a daily basis. Some people recommend taking herbs for a couple of days, then taking a break for a day or two. This has not been my experience. When I take tonic herbs on a daily basis, I feel healthier and stronger. The herbs have a cumulative effect within the body that builds with consistent usage.

When you are sick with a cold or the flu, however, taking a break is a good idea, as tonic herbs might actually strengthen the pathogenic influences within the body. It's also advisable to discontinue use or lower the dose if you experience any side effects. Because tonic herbs are rich, they can be difficult to digest. It may take time for your digestive system to acclimate to the potency of the herbs. If you have, or develop, a sensitive stomach, begin taking tonic herbs in low doses, then gradually increase the dose as your body becomes stronger.

Sometimes, mega-dosing of tonic herbs is necessary. Disease patterns such as cancer and HIV take a tremendous toll on the body. Large doses of herbs can reinforce the healthy energy, or righteous chi, within the body. When dealing with life-

45

threatening diseases, it's essential to work with a licensed acupuncturist or another healthcare provider trained in the use of herbs.

The herbal program is one of the fundamental aspects of harmonizing with the seasons. Once you've decided which herbs to take, make a commitment to taking them regularly. In general, taking herbs twice a day is sufficient. It's most effective to take tonic herbs on an empty stomach, so the body is not digesting anything else at the same time. This allows for maximum absorption of the active ingredients. For those who have a delicate digestive process, it's okay to take herbs with a small amount of food such as rice or a slice of bread.

The Chinese herbs and formulas are powerful. They are safe to take, but *I do not make any medicinal claims*. All of the information in this book is based on thousands of years of accumulated and ancient knowledge from the Chinese masters.[1]

Exercise

 We all know that exercise is an important part of a healthy lifestyle. But how can you exercise so that it helps you become more spiritually connected? You could try yoga or the martial arts, which are great forms of exercise. But if you like to go the gym or enjoy more traditional forms of exercise, where does that leave you? By harmonizing your exercise with the seasons, you will transform your routine into spiritually charged fitness.

Spring and summer are yang seasons, associated with upward and outward energy. So the optimal exercise program for these seasons involves vigorous exercise

---

[1] All of the formulas in this book can be purchased at my website: www.naturesroar.com. All of my products are concentrated liquid extracts that are commercially extracted by my own company. If you prefer, you can buy the individual herbs and prepare them yourself by cooking or extracting them in alcohol. All of the herbs used in these formulas are described in detail in Appendix B.

for extended periods of time. This is the time to sweat, burn, stretch, and tone your body. The autumn and winter months are yin seasons, associated with downward and inward energy. In the yin time of year, the optimal exercise program involves short bursts of strenuous exercises performed with high intensity. This is the time to consolidate, build, and store.

You can do the same exercise program all year round, but I recommend that you adjust the proportions during each season. For example, if you're happy with a combined swimming and weight-lifting program, your workout might involve stretching and warm-up exercises, distance swimming, sprint swimming, weight lifting for endurance, and weight lifting to increase power.

None of these components is eliminated during any particular season. But in the spring you should work out earlier in the morning and emphasize stretching, long-distance swimming, and weight lifting for endurance. You might still do some sprint swimming and weight lifting for power, but you should spend more time on stretching and endurance.

In the summer, this trend continues, but your workout should happen closer to noon. You can spend a little less time on stretching compared to the spring, but you should still spend an ample amount doing stretching exercises. In the summer most of your time should be spent on long-distance swimming and weight lifting for endurance.

In the autumn, your workout should take place in the afternoon. The emphasis is now shifting to sprint swimming and weight lifting for power. Stretching and endurance work continues, but the proportions are adjusted so you spend more time building strength and power.

In the winter you should work out in the evening. This is similar to the autumn workout, but your focus now should be on quick-burst sprinting exercises and weight lifting for building deep strength.

By shifting your workout according to the seasonal cycles, you gain the momentum of nature. It's as if you're riding a natural wave of energy that adds extra zip to your workout and makes you feel more in tune.

Chi Kung

Literally translated, *chi kung* means energy work. This ancient practice contains components of both meditation and exercise. There are many different types of chi  kung, which can be done standing, sitting, or lying down. In each chapter devoted to a season, I will discuss chi kung exercises that can help you to harmonize with that seasonal energy.

Chi kung developed within China's philosophic history. The word *chi* means air, breath, or vital energy. *Kung* is loosely translated as hard work or results achieved over time with effort. Chi kung includes breathing techniques, metal visualization, postures, and slow movements. It is typically practiced on a daily basis; with time and patience, you can develop fabulous states of vitality and well-being using chi kung.

Chi kung is a form of yoga that is some 3,000 to 5,000 years old. Consistent practice can harmonize the chi, strengthen the mind/body/spirit, and prepare the body for long periods of deep meditation. There are literally hundreds of different types of chi kung, including those of Buddhist, Taoist, and Confucian origins. We don't know who originated the practice, but we do know that many of the movements arose from watching animals. There's also a famous tale of the Buddhist monk Bodhidharma, who is credited with bringing Buddhism to China. Bodhidharma is said to have traversed the Himalayas, coming to China from India. Upon receiving a less than favorable reception by the Chinese emperor, Bodhidharma made his way back into the mountains. There, he came upon the Shaolin temple, where he was also not well-received. So, he took up residence in a cave near the temple. The temple monks noticed that Bodhidharma stared at the same rock every day during his meditations. After more than ten years of this, the monks finally took him in as a teacher — after they discovered that Bodhidharma's gaze had bored a hole into his meditation rock. Afterward, so the legend goes, Bodhidharma taught the monks chi kung to strengthen their emaciated bodies.

Within chi kung are several art forms. The two I will discuss here are chi kung proper and *nei kung*. Nei kung (meaning interior work) is the practice of standing or sitting meditation. Chi kung is a fluid and moving art form, whereas nei kung involves little movement. Nei kung builds an energetic structure within the body. Consistent practice can strengthen the legs, open the meridians, optimize posture, and prepare the body to move large quantities of energy. Both practices usually are referred to as chi kung because they are practiced together. Typically, a chi kung session begins with light stretching and warm-up exercises, proceeds to a few minutes of nei kung, then moves to chi kung proper. The workout ends with either sitting or standing meditation. Chi kung usually is practiced in the morning, although it can be done any time.

There are many different types of chi kung, both yin and yang. Yin styles are slower, involve deeper postures, and build energy in the lower body. Designed to slow and consolidate energy, yin styles can combat anxiety and mania. Yang styles, on the other hand, are faster, emphasize stretching, and open the energy flows of the body. Yang forms help to move and express chi, break up stagnation, and relieve depression. During the spring and summer, chi kung exercises emphasizing yang help attune you to the rising and expanding energies of the seasons. In the autumn and winter months, chi kung exercises that are more yin help you to harmonize with the descending and consolidating energies.

If you want to practice chi kung under optimal conditions, there are several concepts you need to know. The first is the *breath*. Breathing is our most basic expres-

49

sion of being alive. How we breathe says a lot about how we live. In chi kung, we breathe slowly and rhythmically, allowing each breath to flow into the deepest part of the belly and then fill the torso from there (see Figure 1). It's as if with each inhalation we fill a golden balloon deep in the lower abdomen. With each inhalation, the balloon inflates to fill the whole torso. With exhalation, the balloon slowly deflates, from the top of the torso down to the lower abdomen. Then the cycle begins again. The breath in basic chi kung comes in through the nose and goes out through the nose.

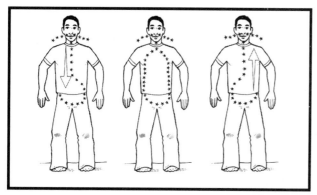

Figure 1

Unless otherwise specified, you should keep the tip of your tongue touching the roof of your mouth during all chi kung and meditation. This way, the tongue connects two powerful energy pathways. One, the *governing vessel*, travels from the perineum up the spine and over the head, ending at the roof of the mouth. The other, the *conception vessel*, continues at the lower jaw and travels down the front of the torso, ending at the perineum. Touching the tongue to the roof of the mouth keeps both of these pathways connected and completes a circuit of energy that flows up the spine, over the head, and down the front of the body. When connected, these two pathways are called the *microcosmic orbit*. They serve to transform dense sexual energy into refined spiritual energy.

Good posture is crucial to chi kung. You must keep your body relaxed when doing chi kung; when a specific posture is called for, it is essential not to strain. Rather, you should allow your body to relax into the posture — even if this takes time.

Standing posture is fundamental. In ancient times, chi kung teachers required their student to do a basic standing posture (nei kung) for two hours at a time for three years, before they learned anything else (See Figure 2). They did this to test the

resolve of their students and to strengthen their bodies. By standing for long periods, the legs become strong, the body learns to relax, and the spine becomes straight. This is vital for chi kung. I am not recommending practice nei kung two hours a day for three years before learning other exercises, but I do recommend some standing practice — as much as you are willing to commit.

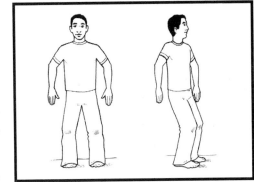

Figure 2

Whether you spend a lot of time standing or not, pay attention to maintaining the optimal posture. Your feet should be straight forward, parallel, and shoulder-

width apart. Bend your knees slightly, keeping your legs strong yet relaxed. Now relax your shoulders. Let your arms hang loosely at your sides, slightly bending them at the elbow. Let your hands relax, with fingers open and palms facing backward. Balance your head over your hips and make sure your spine is straight.

I cannot overemphasize the importance of good posture (see Figure 3). During your practice you must gently yet constantly remind yourself to come back to the correct posture.

Sitting is similar to standing, with the obvious exception that you're seated. The basics remain the same. Sit with your body and shoulders relaxed. Your head should be over your hips and your spine should be straight.

Figure 3

No matter what posture you're in, don't forget to breathe.

As you begin your practice, several visualizations will help you establish an optimal internal environment. Because it's important to be relaxed and happy, the Taoists developed something called the *inner smile*. It starts by visualizing a feeling of warm, glowing happiness at the top of your head. With every breath, this happy energy travels down your body, touching every part of you (see Figure 4).

Next, focus on your feet. Make sure they are firmly planted on the ground, loose and relaxed (see Figure 5). Then allow your weight to sink through your feet into the ground, as if your legs were growing roots into the ground (see Figure 6). From here allow yourself to experience your core. In Taoist yoga, there's a concept known as the *tan tien* (or elixir field). This powerful energy center can be felt once it's been activated. The tan tien is located about three inches below the navel directly in the center of the body (see Figure 7). As you inhale, try to visualize it glowing brightly; as you exhale, see it cool slightly.

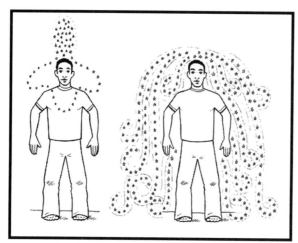

Figure 4

At this point, visualize your energy flowing out through the center of your arms and legs, as if your chi is pouring out through fire hoses (see Figure 8). Then visualize the air around your body becoming thick (see Figure 9).

Sense your whole body weight being supported by this thick air. Now visualize a fishing line sent down from the sky above and hooking to the top of your head. With each breath it pulls you up a bit more, so that your spine becomes erect (see Figure 10). Relax your body and let the chi flow uninhibited.

Figure 5

Figure 6

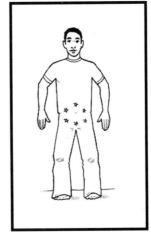

Figure 7

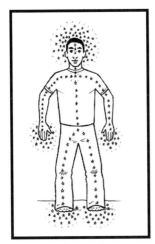

Figure 8

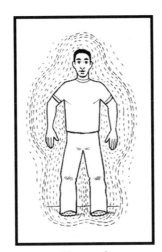

Figure 9

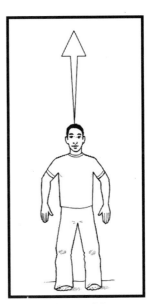

Figure 10

53

Finally, visualize that with each breath your body begins to glow hot, cleansing all impurities; with each exhale, those impurities are released (see Figure 11). Any part of the body, from the organs to the bones, can be used for this exercise.

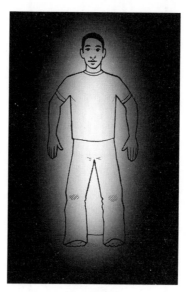

Figure 11

These visualizations help to keep your body relaxed, in proper posture, and functioning while you do chi kung. As you practice, you will learn to cycle through them naturally.

My experience says that learning one exercise well is more important than learning many exercises not so well. Because of this, I will not cover too many exercises in this book. Try to spend time practicing one nei kung and one chi kung exercise. Then do several repetitions of the chi kung. That way you'll learn the subtleties of the exercise and gain an intimate knowledge of the energy it cultivates. There are always more exercises to learn, of course; but if you build a solid foundation, you'll learn those new exercises at a much deeper level.

The Basic Chi Kung Exercise

According to Chinese philosophy, the year (and any complete cycle) is made up of five phases: new yang (wood), full yang (fire), balance (earth), new yin (metal), and full yin (water). The basic chi kung exercise mirrors these five phases. Basic chi kung can be done in the sitting or standing posture. It starts in the basic *nei kung* posture (see Figure 12, page 56, for illustration of the series of movements for the basic chi kung exercise).

First, begin each breath with an inhale (new yang). Let your hands circle in to your lower abdomen and pass up your torso, with the palms up and your fingers pointing toward each other. Now let your hands continue moving up the torso, until they pass your throat. Then begin to turn them, so that your palms rotate toward the front of your body and end up above your head.

If at some point in the movement you have no more room to inhale, simply hold your breath until your hands arrive at their destination. This momentary holding of the breath uses earth energy; this is a practical example of earth energy providing support through the changing cycle.

After you've rotated your hands upward until they've reached their destination above your head, begin to exhale (full yang). As you do so, let your hands sweep out to your sides, palms facing out, hands open, fingers pointing up. At the end of this breath, let your arms come to rest beside your body. If your exhale breath runs out, hold the breath (earth phase) until your hands arrive at their destination. Then begin inhaling (new yin) while your hands rotate so that your palms face up.

With the inhale, let your hands trace the same path they have just come from.

55

Figure 12

When they arrive at the top of your head, rotate the palms face downward and begin to exhale (full yin). Move your hands down past the center of your torso until they reach your lower abdomen, then sweep them out to the sides and back to their original starting position.

This exercise is a microcosm of the larger cycle. Remember, full yin and full yang, although similar, are polar opposites. If you practice this exercise, you'll receive the basic benefits of chi kung and train into your body and mind the intuition of the natural cycle.

56

Introspection — Journaling

Life is an emotion-filled journey, and it's important to spend time looking within at

our emotions and expressing them. Writing in a journal puts us in touch with many aspects of our selves and helps us gain facility in expressing our emotions. Through journal writing we can transform patterns that no longer serve us. In each seasonal chapter I will discuss specific ways you can use journal writing to access and transform unhealthy patterns.

Journal writing encourages the process of self-discovery and growth. You don't have to begin a journal in a particular season. Your writing is for you and you alone; you need not share it with anyone else. Your journal is a space for you to express anything you want, without fear of punishment or critique. Journal writing does not have to be beautiful, exciting, or inspiring. It simply is what comes out of you. There are no pressures to produce or create anything other than what naturally occurs.

It's best to write consistently, every day if possible. But you need to find your own rhythm. There is no set or prescribed amount, simply write until you feel you've expressed your feelings. It's quite common to hit blockages. If you should encounter periods of resistance or obstruction, do your best to lovingly bring yourself back to the process of expression. It is these times that require discipline. For this reason, some people find it helpful to set some sort of schedule for writing. If you are the kind of person who benefits from structure, implement something that works for you. If you are the kind of person who doesn't benefit from structure, do your best to work through any resistive tendencies that emerge.

As you write allow yourself to dialogue with the other voices you may hear. For instance, if you are angry, notice the part of you that is aware of the part that's angry. Allow these two aspects to talk to each other. You might ask, "Anger, what is bothering you?" And the anger might respond, "I'm angry about this or that." You then ask yourself, "What am I *really* angry about?" Often there is something deeper than the superficial anger; as you discover your deeper feelings, you'll have a clearer sense of yourself. When you allow your anger and other feelings to express themselves, you are getting in touch with your truer self. This leads to a state of deeper balance and self-knowledge.

It's also helpful to use the seasons in your journaling work. As the seasons change, notice how different aspects of your psyche become activated. Watch how your internal environment shifts as the days become longer or shorter, as the weather becomes warmer or cooler.

Meditation

Meditation is present in every spiritual tradition known to humankind. In meditation we become deeply introspective and look with absolute honesty at our own lives — a practice that can build kindness and compassion for others and for ourselves. Meditation offers us a safe space to build strength and courage to face our own shortcomings, hurts, and pains.

Meditation can take many forms. Traditionally, it is the practice of intentional breathing and looking within. It might involve journaling, cooking, cross-country skiing, or a host of other practices. The essence of meditation is the consistent practice of becoming quiet. It's simple, yet often quite challenging.

The ancient masters often used meditation in their search for truth. In fact, meditation played a major role in the evolution of Chinese philosophy. Both Taoists and the Buddhists regard meditation as the crown of spiritual discipline. The goal is enlightenment, which is our highest state of awareness combined with our deepest state of interconnectedness with all things.

In the highest levels of enlightenment, we can transcend the limitations of human consciousness and merge with the divine. On a lower level, our meditation allows us to achieve a state of calm tranquility.

To practice meditation, you should first find a quiet place to sit, a place with few or no distractions. You can use many different postures, including the lotus and half lotus positions, sitting in a chair, lying down, or sitting on your knees. Any comfortable position will do, as long as your spine is straight and your body relaxed.

When we meditate, we are attempting to discipline and harmonize the spirit, mind, emotions, and body. Our first tool is *conscious breathing*. As the phrase suggests, conscious breathing involves becoming aware of your breathing cycle. The same principles of breathing discussed earlier (in the section on chi kung) apply to seated meditation. However, during seated meditation there's more emphasis on watching the breath. Conscious breathing can harmonize your chi and quiet your internal environment. As this happens you can observe your inner life, interact with it, and cultivate it.

The most basic form of meditation is the observation of self. This is done by watching what happens during your practice. Watch your breath come in and out of your body. Watch your mind. Watch whatever comes into focus but stay in the neutral position of observing and conscious breathing. Let each thought, feeling, emotion, sensation, and desire float by as a bubble. Don't try to grab the bubble. Instead, let yourself simply watch it float by. If you catch yourself wandering with the bubbles, or if you realize you've stopped breathing, note that you were wandering and return to the neutral state of observation.

Simply observe whatever occurs, but don't become attached to it. You might notice yourself becoming attracted to certain bubbles and repulsed by others. Simply observe yourself. With time, this practice will alter your relationship with yourself and with others. This kind of meditation is a natural process of refining your capacities for compassion, kindness, wisdom, joy, and understanding. Meditation can be challenging, so be gentle with yourself. The rewards are worth it.

Other forms of meditation include visualization, guided meditation, contemplation, mantra, and vocalization.

- *Visualization* is the process of using your mind's eye to picture something. This might be a state, such as being more vital, more confident, or more successful. Visualization also can be used to harmonize with forms of energy, such as planets, phrases, or symbols. Often, visualization is used to open energy centers or meridians within the body, to move energy that's blocked, or to circulate energy through certain pathways.

- *Guided meditation* usually involves someone giving directions on a tape or in a class. It also involves using the mind's eye to picture what is being described. Typically, guided meditations help the audience become more relaxed, more sensitive, or more skillful at meditating. They often involve going on a mental journey. Guided meditation is commonly used to induce various levels of hypnosis.

- *Contemplation* is a more intellectual form of meditation. It involves using the mind to repeatedly focus on an abstract concept such as *"I am."*

- *Mantra meditation* involves the repetitive vocalization of a phrase. This form is used to focus the mind and to develop concentration.

- *Vocalization* (or sounding) is a basic form of mantra meditation. It involves a more intuitive expression of sound. This form often is used to release blocked emotions from the body.

This list is just a small sample of the many kinds of meditation available.

With consistent practice, we can use meditation to attain a clear mind, a more positive outlook, and a healthier body. The practice can help us to settle emotions, resolve dysfunctional life patterns, and relieve stress. Meditation practice also can improve our ability to perceive energy — a process called *opening the psychic senses*. Some truly gifted individuals actually are psychic. However, most people who call themselves psychics have merely cultivated deeper levels of sensitivity and awareness.

In each chapter on a season, I will discuss specific meditations you can do to harmonize with the seasonal energies.

Chapter 4

Putting it All Together

Now that we've examined the five elements and all the tools available to us, how do we actually use them to achieve seasonal harmony?

Balancing Energies

The best way to harmonize with the energy of the seasons is to balance several energies at one time. Harmonizing with the energy of the season you are in is called *entrainment*. Entraining is the process of lining up your energy with another energy. A simple way to understand this is to walk behind someone and copy his or her walk. You might notice that your posture, gait, attitude, breathing, and viewpoint change. By entraining with the seasonal energy, you become connected to the pattern of the energy. The energy pattern of your body, mind, and spirit begins to copy the way the seasonal energy flows.

It's also wise to balance the energy of the current season with its polar opposite. This is called *oppositional harmony*. For example, during the winter the weather is cold and the natural energy is deep and slow. So you'll want to go deep within yourself and harmonize with the seasonal energy that is present (entrainment). But it's important not to freeze or deprive your system of the fire it needs to keep warm and perform its metabolic tasks (oppositional). This balance between entrainment and oppositional energy will become one of the gauges of your level of overall harmony.

So, to achieve seasonal harmony, you must balance yourself between the season you're in and its polar opposite. This balance applies to all the tools you use, including diet, herbs and supplements, exercise, chi kung, and meditation. So, for example, in the summer seasonal wisdom says you should take herbs and supplements that protect the heart (summer) and nourish the shen. At the same time, however, you should supply the kidneys (winter) with herbs to strengthen the jing and balance the summer entrainment. Keeping the kidneys involved in the process of summer harmony helps the body become more deeply rooted; this alignment then becomes integrated into the whole system. Adhering to this important principle makes the process of seasonal harmony much more effective.

Earth Energy

Earth energy also plays a crucial role in this process. The earth is the center and has many important functions within the body, including governing the digestive system (see Chapter 7). It's a good idea always to keep the earth involved in the process of seasonal harmony. On a practical level, you do this by keeping your digestive system healthy and balanced. Throughout the year try to include earth tools in your practice: Make earth foods part of your diet, include an earth formula in your herbal program, do earth exercises, and practice earth meditations. In Chapter 7, I will discuss the functions and responsibilities of the earth. For now, simply note that the earth is a major piece of the puzzle.

The seasonal changes are subtle rather than sweeping or abrupt. Because they are in constant motion, flowing with the seasons is a little like trying to hit a moving target. So your seasonal modifications must be gentle, gradual, based on proportions

63

and an understanding that what is here today will be transformed into something new tomorrow. These gentle adjustments help the body attune to changes in temperature, sun exposure, and other factors that can stress the immune system. It's important to keep your mind flexible, allowing the process to evolve organically.

As you begin the process of seasonal harmony, know that your whole being will be affected. You might notice changes on different levels, but remember that the system is really one whole. The longer you practice, the more your whole being will become integrated. It is a slow, gradual process, so be patient.

PART II

The Phases and Seasons

Chapter 5

Spring

SPRING IS THE SEASON of birth and beginning, the time when the earth and all its inhabitants are renewed after the winter slumber. Flowers begin to bloom, leaves begin to bud on the trees, and vitality increases. Within the five phases, spring symbolized by the energy of *wood*, is characterized as the potential energy stored within the seed. It's the power of the seedling to push its roots down through the soil in search of water, while pushing its stem up toward the sun. In general, spring is the time when all natural energy moves upward and outward. We experience this same pattern within our bodies. Our creativity, vitality, repressed emotions, and stored toxins all begin to express themselves in spring.

The Liver and the Wood Element

The organ systems most related to the spring are the liver (yin) and gall bladder (yang). The liver has many important functions in the body, extending to both the physical and emotional levels. It is in charge of moving and harmonizing energy, blood, and emotions. It controls the amount of tension and relaxation in the body,

67

and nourishes the eyes, the nails, and the tendons. The liver also governs the female menstrual system.

The liver is in charge of harmonizing chi and ensuring that it flows smoothly throughout the body. If the liver is functioning well, chi will flow through the body, the meridians, and the organs in a harmonious way. The smooth flow of chi supports the natural functions of our organs. If chi is flowing smoothly, we tend to be in a good mood; we are motivated, our internal functions are smooth, and we are in a general state of good health. If the liver is not functioning well and chi is stagnant or blocked, we tend to be in a bad mood, have difficulty getting motivated, and be in a less than optimal state of health.

The liver filters and removes impurities from the blood. Everything that enters the body eventually finds its way to the blood. Once a substance enters the blood, it passes through the liver to be metabolized and excreted. The more complex a molecule is, the more difficult it is for the liver to metabolize. Consuming too many complex molecules, such as pharmaceutical drugs, decreases the liver's functional capacity.

The liver also is in charge of harmonizing our emotions. Remember, in Chinese philosophy there is no separation between body and mind. If chi flows smoothly, our emotions are tranquil. If chi flows erratically or is blocked, our emotional energy will manifest in the same way.

The liver has a wide emotional spectrum and is intimately connected with creativity, expression, faith, and the force of growth. When the creative energy in the body is allowed to express itself fully, the liver will be healthy. Positive emotions associated with the liver are hope, faith, trust, creativity, direction, and the ability to effectively process stress and relax. When the liver is blocked from expressing itself effectively, it functions less than optimally. Negative emotions associated with the liver are anger, frustration, resentment, tension, hopelessness, blocked creativity, a lack of trust or direction, the inability to express oneself fully, process stress, or relax. Of all the emotions, anger and frustration have the strongest negative effects on the liver. These emotions are powerful signs that creativity and other natural forces are not achieving expression. If you can discover the underlying causes of your anger and frustration, you will be able to apply the tremendous force those emotions carry toward accomplishing your true goals.

Kahlil Gibran's masterpiece *The Prophet* includes a vignette that eloquently describes the psychological aspect of the wood element and the liver.

> And a woman spoke, saying, Tell us of Pain. And he said: Your pain is the breaking of the shell that encloses your understanding. Even as the stone of the fruit must break that its heart may stand in the sun, so must you know pain. And could you keep your heart in wonder at the daily miracles of your life, your pain would not seem less wondrous than your joy; And you would accept the seasons of your heart, even as you have always accepted the seasons that pass over your fields. And you would watch with serenity through the winters of your grief.
>
> Much of your pain is self-chosen. It is the bitter potion by which the physician within you heals your sick self. Therefore trust the physician, and drink his remedy in silence and tranquility: For his hand, though heavy and hard, is guided by the tender hand of the unseen, And the cup he brings, though it burn your lips, has been fashioned of the clay which the potter has moistened with his own sacred tears.

This story profoundly illustrates the power of the liver energy and the wood element. It speaks of having faith in the great unseen potter, of the magnificence of creation, and of trust in the process of life. The shen (spirit) resides in the heart, and the liver is closely connected with our trust in the spiritual. Having faith in the unseen seems contradictory. How can you trust something you can't see? That is the paradox. Because to live in harmony with the cycles of life and nature, we must have faith in that which we cannot classify or quantify. We must trust the unseen force that moves through, governs, and maintains the whole of creation. Learning to let it guide us is the lesson of the wood element.

The liver moderates the amount of tension within the body. That's why the liver is said to have a role in regulating the nervous system. When the liver is functioning well, it can tense and relax parts of the body as needed. When the liver is impaired, it can't regulate this action and the body has excessive tension. The parts of the body most susceptible to tension are areas that the meridians of the liver or gall bladder pass through: These are the head, neck, sides of the torso, lower abdomen, genitalia, hips, outside of the thighs, and feet. This is why your neck and head will feel tense after a stressful day.

The liver is said to nourish and control the function of the eyes. When the liver is functioning well, plenty of blood and nourishing energy is sent to the eyes. When the liver is not functioning well, less energy is available. A symptom of dysfunction within the eyes typically is seen as a disharmony within the liver. Because alcohol and drugs cause the liver to become overheated, their effect appears as redness in the eyes.

The liver is in charge of nourishing tendons, ligaments, muscles, sinews, the toe- and fingernails, and all of the body's connective tissue. TCM practitioners believe that the liver blood nourishes the connective tissue. The phrase "liver blood" is a way of describing the strength, health, and nourishing effectiveness of the blood. When the liver is healthy, it keeps the blood clean and vitalized. If there is ample liver blood, the body's connective tissue receives proper nourishment and is pliable and resilient. If the liver blood is impaired or deficient, it can't nourish the connective tissue. At this point, the tendons will contract and be stiff and slower to heal.

The liver also is responsible for regulating the menstrual system. If a woman's liver energy is functioning well, her periods will come on a regular schedule, with a normal variation of a day or so, and with little or no discomfort. The flow will be within "normal" parameters (because every woman's body is different, establishing normal parameters is difficult), there will no clotting, and the period will last four to five days. If her liver energy is dysfunctional and not flowing well, however, her periods may be erratic and accompanied by moderate to severe cramping. There may be odd flow patterns, with or without clotting, and the periods may vary from the four-to five-day average. Harmonizing and nourishing the liver can help in balancing the menstrual cycle. It is important to treat whatever blockages exist, including emotions and stagnant or deficient blood or chi.

Heavy foods, excessive consumption of drugs or alcohol, toxic environments, anger, stress, grief or depression, chronic or acute illness, lack of sleep, overwork, and other lifestyle imbalances can damage the liver and inhibit its ability to function properly.

The liver is particularly susceptible to dysfunctions of stagnation and heat. Liver chi stagnation is one of the most common disharmonies in Chinese medicine. It can be caused by any of the factors listed above, and is a sign that the liver energy is not flowing effectively. A hot liver also is common. This is a sign that the relative balance of yin and yang has been disturbed. The liver is a complex organ and requires considerable attention to remain balanced. It needs the right proportions of coolness, movement, and relaxation to operate in an optimal way.

You can work on the liver at any time of the year. However, in the spring you'll find the most natural energy available to strengthen and harmonize the liver and its many functions.

Tools for Spring

In order to harmonize with the energy of spring, we must *feel* the seasonal change. Notice how the outer world changes with the seasons, and how the internal environment responds. Then, take actions to support the movement you perceive — actions such as modifying your diet, establishing an herbal program and an exercise program, and meditating. It's also important to detoxify your body, clean out your living space, and resolve any interpersonal conflicts — hence the phrase "spring cleaning." The purpose of this cleansing is to create the space that will allow vitality and creativity to flourish.

When harmonizing the liver, it is not uncommon for emotions, memories, or feelings that have been buried to resurface. This is natural as the energy of spring begins to rise.

Case Study: Liver/Face

Kevin, age thirty-one, was a successful executive in the entertainment industry. After several years of working under intense stress, he developed Bell's palsy-like symptoms. The right side of his face became numb and drooped as he lost muscular control. That's when he came to see me. After we had talked for a while, he mentioned that he had difficulty breathing and clearing his mind, and that he felt a lot of tension in his ribs. He also had considerable neck and shoulder tightness and pain. Kevin had been quite athletic, and these issues were limiting his ability to be physically active.

All of these symptoms validated my intuition that his liver energy had become stagnant and overwhelmed. We talked about the energy of the liver and its special visibility during springtime. I explained the basic theory and recommended that he modify his diet, making it much lighter. I suggested that he cut back on meat and chicken and eat mainly fish with a lot of greens.

Then our conversation turned to emotions, and the liver's role in them. Kevin had a powerful social presence, but he seemed stuck when it came to matters of the heart. I suggested that he begin journaling to get in touch with his emotions.

As we discussed exercises for harmonizing the liver, he became quite intrigued. I recommended that he increase his stretching before workouts and mentioned that yoga classes would be beneficial. I also suggested that he begin taking my herbal formula "Rhythm" (see page 80) to harmonize and open his liver energy. Finally, I recommended that he take at least a few minutes each day to walk outside and clear his mind. Before he left, I performed an acupuncture treatment to open his liver energy.

The next week when I saw Kevin he seemed a bit lighter in spirit. He said the previous session had gotten a lot of things moving in him. He still had pain in his neck and shoulders, and his face still showed palsy symptoms, but he felt a little better. He had made changes in his diet, taken the herbs, and gone to a few yoga classes. He had not yet started to journal, but he said that he knew the writing was important. I gave him another treatment.

The next week Kevin reported that he felt significantly better. There was improvement in his face and neck and shoulders. He had continued with the diet, herbs, and yoga, and had even written in his journal a couple of times. "I realize I've been carrying a lot of emotional baggage," he said, "but I didn't know it could have such a strong influence over my health."

A week later Kevin reported continuing improvement. He had regained some feeling in his face, and a lot of the drooping had dissipated. He had even regained some control of his facial muscles. He reported spending a lot of time writing in his journal, noting, "I feel as if I purged something that was stuck in me."

I continued seeing Kevin for a few more weeks and each time he reported generally feeling better. He began coming in every other week, then once a month. Today,

73

he continues with the program, keeps his diet light, takes his herbs regularly, exercises with the seasonal principles in mind, and occasionally writes in his journal.

Diet

In the spring, as the depth and heaviness of winter give way to the sun and awakening of nature, the optimal diet is one of general cleansing. Dietary modifications for spring include lighter foods such as vegetables (especially leafy green vegetables, steamed or eaten raw), light soups, and fish. Vegetables are relatively easy to digest, they are of the earth, and they help the body regenerate. Many vegetables have medicinal and tonic effects on the body. In addition, they are rich sources of essential vitamins, minerals, roughage, and fiber. Eating vegetables stimulates and cleanses the colon, and this aids in the process of detoxification. You should eat vegetables all year long, but especially in the spring they should make up a larger proportion of your overall diet. Table 5 lists several vegetables and their cleansing effects on the body.

During the spring it's preferable to choose foods and meals that are easy to digest. This allows the body to be free, flowing, and unburdened by the heaviness of large, rich meals. Use oils, sauces, and other food flavorings that are light and digestible. Another important dietary adjustment is a gradual but dramatic decrease of overall food intake. In particular, it's wise to eliminate meat altogether and substitute fish. You should try to eat smaller meals four or five times a day, eating until the stomach is only about eighty percent full. By maintaining a slightly hungry state, you don't overburden your body's digestive process. The spring diet is designed to encourage the seasonal rising of the body's energy and to aid the body in the process of detoxification.

Spring is a great time to include fresh vegetable juices in your diet. Be careful, however, to heed the Chinese maxim, "All things in moderation." Juices, salads, and other raw vegetables are cooling or cold. Eating them makes the digestive fire work hard, first to warm up the food you eat, and then to digest it. Try to balance cooling raw foods and juices with warming soups, cooked meals, and hot teas.

The color associated with the wood element and spring is green. Many green foods and supplements detoxify the liver, build the blood, and rejuvenate the body. In addition, green foods help calm and refresh the body, mind, and spirit. Green vegetables are rich in chlorophyll — the substance that makes plants green — which is nourishing, refreshing, detoxifying, and cleansing. Chlorophyll helps the body build and oxygenate blood, renew tissue, and improve liver function. Green foods help your body harmonize with the energy of spring.

The general trend of energy during the spring is to rise and disperse, and food preparation can enhance this action. Cooking food for short times preserves its natural dispersing quality and keeps the energy of the food light and superficial. Steaming, blanching, quick frying, and other fast-cooking methods are preferable, but grilling and barbecuing also are good choices.

Each season is associated with a particular taste, and the sour taste is commonly connected with spring. The sour is balanced by the pungent flavor. The sour taste has an astringent action that consolidates energy, whereas pungency has a moving and dispersing action within the body. You should include both of these tastes in balanced amounts during the spring. Although traditionally associated with the fire element and summer, the bitter flavor also is consumed in large quantities in the spring, because many green foods have a bitter taste.

Vegetable	Properties	Actions
Beet	Sweet taste, neutral temperature	Purifies the blood, detoxifies and tonifies the liver, and calms the shen.
Broccoli	Pungent and bitter taste, cool temperature	Clears excess heat, detoxifies the body, and calms the shen.
Cabbage	Sweet and pungent taste, neutral temperature	Calms the stomach; the juice is used to treat ulcers.
Carrot	Sweet taste, neutral temperature	Strengthens the lungs, the spleen, and the liver; eliminates waste and detoxifies.
Cauliflower	Sweet taste, neutral temperature	Nourishes the spleen, drains dampness, clears the intestines, and detoxifies the body.
Celery	Sweet and bitter taste, cooling temperature	Clears heat, detoxifies, and calms the liver.
Chard	Bitter taste, cool temperature	Calms the emotions, relieves stress and tension, clears excessive heat from the blood, and detoxifies the body.
Cucumber	Sweet taste, cooling temperature	Clears excessive heat, calms the shen, detoxifies the body, and replenishes body fluids.
Daikon radish	Bitter taste, cool temperature	Detoxifies the body, cools the liver, promotes the secretion of digestive fluids, and purifies the blood.
Garlic	Pungent taste, hot temperature	Vigorously warms and detoxifies the body, moves stagnant energy, and is anti-microbial.
Kale	Sweet and bitter taste, neutral temperature	Clears and improves the liver function and calms the shen.

Table 5

Lettuce	Bitter and sweet taste, neutral temperature	Detoxifies the body, clears excessive heat, and calms the shen.
Mustard green	Bitter taste, cool temperature	Cools the liver and the blood, clears excessive heat and phlegm, and activates the circulation of chi.
Onion	Pungent taste, warm temperature	Warms the body, removes stagnant energy, and strengthens the lungs.
Radish	Pungent and sweet taste, cool temperature	Detoxifies the body, clears and strengthens the lungs, and removes food stagnation.
Spinach	Sweet taste, cool temperature	Builds and detoxifies the blood, strengthens the liver, and promotes healthy bowel activity.
Dandelion green	Bitter taste, cool temperature	Detoxifies the body, cools the blood, clears the liver, and promotes the flow of liver chi.
Sprout	Sweet taste, cool temperature	Gently promotes upward and outward movement of the chi, clears the liver, and cools the blood.
Tomato	Sweet and sour taste, neutral temperature	Detoxifies the liver, the blood, and the body as a whole and strengthens weakened digestive energy.
Burdock root	Bitter and pungent taste, cool temperature	Promotes detoxification; clears damp, eczema, and rashes; dispels wind heat; and stimulates digestion.
Lotus root	Sweet taste, cool temperature	Clears heat, quenches thirst, relieves irritability, cools the blood, and strengthens the stomach.
Watercress	Pungent, bitter, and sweet taste, cool temperature	Drains dampness; promotes urination; detoxifies the body; cools, clears, and nourishes the lungs; and promotes secretion of digestive fluids.

Table 5, continued

Listed below are some basic food principles for spring:

1. **Steamed vegetables.** Pick your favorite green vegetables, cut them up, and steam them. Be sure to save the water that's left after the steaming, as it's a rich source of vitamins and minerals. You can drink the steaming water on the spot or use it as a base for a soup or rice dish.

2. **Salads.** It's easy to get an assortment of lettuces and greens in salads. You can buy already packaged gourmet greens or make your own mixes. Experiment with different vegetables, fruits, nuts, and even a bit of cheese. Use color, texture, and taste to keep salads fresh and interesting. Don't go overboard with the cheese or other heavy foods; the goal is to keep the salad light and refreshing.

3. **Soups.** Spring soups should be light and refreshing. Vegetable stock, fish stock, and a little chicken stock are the main foundations. You can also use the water left over from steaming vegetables. Include your favorite chopped vegetables and rice. Remember to cook thicker root vegetables longer. Add the leafier vegetables at the end to preserve their texture and prevent wilting. Again, try different colors and combinations for variety.

4. **Fish.** Any fish you like is a fine choice. The marinade and cooking method give the fish its distinction. In the spring, pan-frying and outdoor grilling are great ways of cooking. Use a marinade that incorporates the spices, tastes, and colors of spring. In general, light and fresh marinades are preferable. Soy sauce, teriyaki sauce, and fruit juices are good bases to start with. Chop in garlic, other vegetables, or fruits to give more complexity to the taste. Activating pungent spices such as turmeric, oregano, and basil are good in the spring, as they make fish easier to digest and also taste good. Don't overdo it, though — spices can be drying and tend to imbalance the yin and yang. Table 6 lists some common spices and their actions in the body.

Spice	Properties	Actions
Basil	Pungent taste, warm temperature	Warms digestion and dries dampness.
Black pepper (freshly ground)	Pungent taste, hot temperature	Warms the body, warms digestion, and disperses chi; also has antibiotic properties.
Cardamom	Pungent taste, warm temperature	Warms digestion and dries dampness.
Cayenne pepper	Pungent taste, hot temperature vitamin C.	Warms the body, disperses chi, and dries dampness; has antibiotic properties; is high in
Cinnamon	Pungent taste, warm temperature	Warms the body, enhances circulation, dries dampness, and promotes urination.
Cloves	Pungent taste, warm temperature	Warms the body, activates digestion, and dries dampness.
Garlic	Pungent taste, hot temperature	Warms the body, disperses chi, dries dampness, and invigorates wei chi; also has antibiotic properties.
Ginger	Pungent taste, warm temperature	Warms digestion and soothes the digestive process.
Oregano	Pungent taste, warm temperature	Warms digestion and dries dampness.
Sea salt	Salty taste, cool temperature	Cools and nourishes the body; replenishes and regulates body fluids.
Thyme	Pungent taste, warm temperature	Warms digestion and dries dampness.

Table 6

Herbal Formula: "Rhythm"

The Nature's Roar™ custom formula "Rhythm" helps to harmonize the liver, moving the liver chi and allowing the liver energy rise with the upward flow of spring. It also helps your emotions transform in a harmonious procession. This formula was designed to relax the body and mind, ease tension, and help you to move more easily through the challenges of life. You can take "Rhythm" throughout the year to strengthen your liver, or only take it from March 21 to June 21 to harmonize your liver system with the opening of spring. The formula includes bulpeurum, peony, astragalus, dang gui, schizandra, and reishi.

Case Study: Liver

Peggy, age thirty-six, came to see me because of recurring severe migraine headaches. A tall, big-boned woman, she moved with slow deliberation. She reported that once

a month for about a day or two she would be incapacitated by pain, sensitivity to light, and nausea. She reported that, while her periods were relatively regular, they brought considerable pain and cramping. Because of this, I considered it likely that the source of her migraines was deep liver chi stagnation —what Western medicine would call hormonal imbalance. Not only did her symptoms suggest this, her slow movements and large size added to her propensity for energy stagnation.

Unfortunately, it was not spring, so we could not directly ride the wave of spring energy. But we could use many other tools, starting with a change in diet. I suggested that she add a lot of steamed green vegetables, which are easy to digest, light, and mildly detoxifying. I also recommended that she eat less meat and more fish. Cutting down on dairy products was another suggestion.

I asked Peggy to begin yoga three to five times a week, because the stretching and breathing are good for opening and freeing the liver chi. I also asked her to take daily long walks, to clear her mind and move her liver chi. And I recommended that she begin taking my herbal formula "Rhythm" to balance and open her liver chi.

I told her she should begin journaling as often as she could manage. People with deep liver chi stagnation, both men and women, often have emotions bound into the pattern. Journaling is a great way to identify and express those emotions. Finally, I gave her an acupuncture treatment designed to open her liver energy.

Peggy did much of what I recommended. She included many more steamed vegetables in her diet and cut out much of the meat. She started going to a yoga class once or twice a week, taking long walks several times a week, and journaling about three times a week. "I had no idea that the emotional hurt I experienced earlier in life could contribute to my migraines," she said. She also began taking the herbs twice a day.

After two weeks, I saw Peggy again. She reported that not much had changed, but she did seem to have more energy and was able to think a little more clearly. In the two weeks since her first visit she had not had a migraine. I gave her another treatment and urged her to continue the program.

Two weeks later, I saw her for the third time. She said she'd had a migraine during those two weeks, but that the intensity was much less and the duration shorter. This trend was exciting to her, and she became more motivated to stick with the program.

I saw Peggy every two weeks for about three months. During that time she continued with her lifestyle changes. Although the migraines didn't completely disappear, their intensity and duration continued to diminish. I urged her to continue what she was doing and, with the arrival of spring, to really focus on opening her liver energy. I recommended that she thoroughly clean her house, her car, and her work area with the arrival of spring.

81

Once spring had passed, I called Peggy to see how she was doing. She reported that much in her life had changed and she felt much healthier and more alive. She had begun going to school in the evening and was preparing to change careers. Her marriage, she said, seemed to be going more smoothly. She also told me that she now had migraines only about once every three months, rather than every month. Their intensity was minor and the duration only a couple of hours. She was continuing with many of my recommendations, and said she now enjoyed spending her free time journaling, doing yoga, and going for long walks with her husband.

Exercise

Spring is a time of new yang, and the basic energetic theme is rising energy. The best kinds of exercise for spring are those that get the energy moving, build a good sweat, and stretch the muscles and tendons. The Chinese classics suggest waking with the rising sun and taking long, brisk walks. Important concepts for spring exercise are waking up early to exercise, doing exercises that help the body cleanse and release stored waste, and doing fairly strenuous exercise for extended periods of time.

The liver rules the tendons, ligaments, muscles, and connective tissue. Therefore, spring is a good time to do stretching exercises that are long, deep, and sweat-inducing. While many forms of yoga are good for this, *ashtanga yoga* is probably the best. It combines movement with deep postures and works up a vigorous sweat. Other beneficial exercises include hiking, martial arts (especially forms that work up a sweat), swimming, running, skating, and biking. Weight lifting also is an acceptable exercise for spring, as long as you focus on good technique. Concentrate on stretching the muscles through their full range of motion and do more repetitions with less weight.

Adapting your exercise program to use the principles of spring can move your liver chi, cleanse your body, and help you develop a deeper sense of motivation, hope, and faith.

Exercise	Modifications for spring
Hiking	Walk on flatter trails for longer distances, and increase your stretching.
Martial arts	Concentrate on stretching and more repetitions of movements.
Weight lifting	Use more repetitions and less weight, and increase the amount of stretching you do.
Running	Run longer distances and slower speeds and spend more time stretching.

Chi Kung

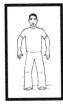

During the spring it's best to do chi kung exercises that balance the liver, move the liver chi, stretch the ribs, and open the liver and gall bladder meridians. The nei kung posture for the spring starts in the basic posture (see Figure 13). Stretch your arms high above your head, with your palms facing up and your fingers pointing in toward each other. Keep your shoulder and elbow joints open and not locked. Stretching your arms above your head opens your rib cage, stretches your internal organs, and improves blood flow to your liver. This posture can help release trapped emotions and stagnant energy.

Inhale through your nose with your mouth closed and your tongue touching the roof of your mouth. Then exhale through your mouth and let your tongue come off the roof of your mouth. This is known as a cleansing breath; it helps to disperse

Figure 13

83

excess energy and in this posture it moves and expresses chi. You can enhance the cleansing power of the exercise by adding a sound as you exhale. According to traditional Taoist practice, each organ has an associated sound, as listed in Table7.

Organ	Color	Sound
Liver	Green	*Shhuuu*
Heart	Red	*Haaaaa*
Spleen	Yellow	*Whoooo*
Lungs	White	*Ssshhh*
Kidneys	Black/dark blue	*Fffuuu*

Table 7

Allow the sounds to be expressed as vibrations. Let them resonate throughout your body, especially through the associated organ. Don't limit yourself to just one sound. Spring is a great time to detoxify all of your organs. Vocalize whatever sounds feel appropriate, allowing your intuition to guide the release and expression of emotions and stagnant energy. As you become comfortable with the practice of vocalization, you might want to visualize the organ being filled with its color.

The chi kung exercise for spring is the first half of the basic chi kung exercise (see Chapter 3). It begins in the basic chi kung posture (see Figure 14). Inhale through your nose, sweep your hands toward your lower abdomen, then raise them up the center of your body, keeping them six inches in front of the body with the fingers almost touching. As your hands pass your throat area, begin to rotate the palms out toward the direction you are facing. Continue to move them up through the center of your body until your arms are extended straight above your head. At this point, your inhale is complete. If you run out of lung space along the way, just hold the breath and use some earth energy. As you exhale through your mouth (cleansing breath), move your hands out to the sides in a circular motion with your arms extended. The movement finishes when your hands arrive at the point where the exercise began. This basic spring chi kung exercise is designed to activate the liver chi, cleanse stagnant chi, release trapped emotions, and entrain with the movement of spring.

Figure 14

As with the spring nei kung, adding vocalization intensifies the cleansing power of the exercise. In general, the pace of this exercise is slow, although you may want to experiment with changing the speed. Make sure the speed of your movements matches the length of your breathing cycle. Do as many repetitions as time allows.

Journaling

The wood element is the beginning of the journey through the seasons. It speaks of

birth and early growth. Wood energy often triggers feelings of inspiration to start something new and offers bursts of fresh energy and direction. As you begin the process of journaling, you'll be working with wood energy. In this part of the cycle, you might encounter blockage, resistance, anger, frustration, hostility, shame, blame, jealousy, judgment, and criticism. As you work through whatever needs to be expressed, you'll begin to uncover such feelings as hope, faith, inspiration, drive, true desire, and flow. Each time you get in touch with a new layer of feelings, you become more in tune with your truer feelings. Beginning to explore the inner self can be difficult, and the process often involves two steps forward and one step back. Don't worry about this, just keep writing. Allowing yourself to express any thoughts, feelings, emotions, or past experiences that come up paves the way for a clear understanding of who you truly are. Writing helps dissolve the confusion that makes it difficult to act from a centered place. The more you write, the more change you will see.

As you grow more comfortable with this process, allow yourself to see the areas where you may be blocked. Each time you find a blockage, allow yourself to talk to the blocked feelings. Talk to them as you would talk to a friend, and find out what is wrong with them. Ask yourself what you gain from staying blocked. What safety is in that state? What do you need to become unblocked. What fears do you associate with being unblocked?

Ask yourself these same kinds of questions each time you contact other thoughts, feelings, or past experiences. Simply see that they are there, and allow them to express whatever they need to.

Meditation

The meditation for spring can be done in a lotus or half-lotus posture, a seated posture, sitting on the knees, or while walking. Allow your breath to flow in through your nose, with your tongue touching the roof of your mouth; then allow it to flow out through your mouth as you drop your tongue. Keep your eyes opened slightly, and focus your gaze on an object of your choice. If the space is conducive, add an

affirmation to your exhalation. Affirmations in the spring are statements that affirm the positive emotional qualities of the liver. These include *I trust*, *I am motivated*, and *I believe*. The spring meditation is designed to release energy or emotions that are stuck, stored, or stagnant. Whatever you come in contact with, give it expression. You may want to keep your journal close by so you can write down any thoughts, feelings, or emotions that emerge. Be patient and don't force the process.

Chapter 6

Summer

Continue the practice for as long as time permits.

SUMMER IS THE time of maturation to fullness, when the earth is in full bloom. Fruit trees are heavy with fruit, days are long, and we feel at our most vital. The season of summer is symbolized within the five phases by the energy of fire, the full expression of nature's energy. Above all, fire has the power to emit light and warmth. Throughout the spring our natural energy rises and expands; with the transition to summer, our energy moves upward and outward to its peak. It feels as if an energy faucet is turned on in the spring. As summer arrives, that faucet is opened all the way, allowing our energy to flow freely. Summer is the full manifestation of yang energy.

The Heart and the Fire Element

The organ systems most related to summer are the heart (yin) and the small intestine (yang). The heart is the most refined energy system in the body. TCM considers the heart the king of bodily systems. The shen, or spirit, is stored in the heart. Because the shen is our higher nature, the functioning of our heart is intimately linked with our outlook on life. While the heart has many functions within the body, the Chinese recognized that, without the illumination of the shen, we would have little to differentiate us from the beasts.

The duties of the heart are divided into physical and subtle functions. On the physical level, heart energy rules the cardiovascular system. The subtle functions of the heart involve the shen, which governs our ability to see beyond the dualistic illusion of life to the oneness of all things. The shen maintains our emotional equilibrium, governs the clarity of our thought, and oversees our ability to achieve restful sleep.

The cardiovascular system (the physical aspect of the heart) includes the structures of the heart muscle and the blood vessels, both venous and arteriole, as well as the functions of pumping the blood through the body and maintaining the integrity of blood vessels. The function of the heart can be felt in the pulse and seen in the color of the face. When your heart is functioning well, your blood circulation is smooth, your pulse is vigorous, and your face has a healthy luster. If your heart becomes weakened, your blood circulation is impaired, your pulse may be weak or erratic, and your face may look pale and lusterless.

The heart energy system stores the shen and rules our higher awareness. The shen is the most refined part of our being — part spirit, part emotion, and part intellect. It is the aspect that, undaunted by the stresses of life, sees the bigger picture, is in tune with the sublime rhythms of the universe, and appreciates the value of life. When the heart energy system is balanced and healthy, the shen is able to open and evolve.

One purpose of consistent meditation is to help the body and the heart relax. As the body relaxes, the shen opens. The phrases "open hearted" and "big hearted"

89

reflect the opening of the shen. As the shen opens, we can see that, although the world manifests itself in duality, all things are ultimately one. At its highest stage, the opening of shen brings enlightenment. Enlightened beings are literally so filled with light that they radiate love and joy. Acts of kindness, generosity, sharing, compassion, caring, and love all arise from the shen. Prayer, yoga, meditation, spiritual practice, chi kung, and other practices that bring calm introspection cultivate the shen.

The heart is responsible for overseeing and maintaining emotional balance within the body. When the heart is functioning well, it allows each emotion its proper expression and provides an overriding mechanism when an emotion becomes out of balance. If the heart is not functioning well, the emotions run free. Without the heart's balancing influence, emotions are allowed expression, whether appropriate or not.

The heart also controls the power and clarity of the intellect. When your heart functions well, your intellect is clear and sharp, and responds quickly and effectively. However, if your heart becomes deficient, your mind may be muddled and unable to respond quickly and effectively.

The heart is responsible for the quality of sleep. When your heart is calm and functioning well, your shen is able to rest peacefully and your body follows suit. But if your heart is agitated, your shen may have a hard time coming to rest, and sleeping may be difficult. If the heart is deficient of blood, it's hard to maintain sleep. If the heart is deficient of yin, you will have difficulty falling asleep. If the heart is deficient of both blood and yin, you'll have a hard time both falling asleep and staying asleep.

Positive emotional aspects of the heart are joy and love. When the heart is balanced, our emotions tend to be smooth and appropriately expressed, and we have a general sense of joyfulness. Negative emotional aspects of the heart are anxiety, mania, and — at worst — insanity. When the heart becomes unbalanced, our emotions tend to be erratic and inappropriately expressed, and we feel an overriding sense of anxiety. In extreme cases of heart imbalance, we see such disharmonies as bipolar disorder, schizophrenia, and other forms of psychosis.

Frank Capra's film *It's a Wonderful Life* beautifully illustrates the concepts of the fire element. The movie tracks the life of George Bailey (played by Jimmy Stewart). As we watch George grow, we see his tremendous desire to travel the world and build cities of the future. A series of events, however, keep him at home to run the business his father started, the Building and Loan Association. The Building and Loan is the only town institution not owned by the villain, Mr. Potter. As George's life unfolds, we see all the sacrifices he makes in order to keep the Building and Loan alive. At a critical point, George's business partner, Uncle Billy is about to make the year-end deposit at the bank of $8,000. Just then, the evil Mr. Potter comes into the bank. Uncle Billy becomes distracted, and the $8,000 accidentally falls into Potter's hands. This loss starts a series of events that eventually results in George standing on a bridge contemplating suicide. But Clarence, George's guardian angel, appears in the nick of time to give George a view of what life in the town would have been like if he had never been born. George gets to see how much good he has done and realizes how wonderful his life really is.

This movie can be seen as a study of the fire element, and how the heart must reconcile its pure artistic desires with the difficulty of implementing those desires in the real world. Even though George wants to be free to travel and build, he is needed to maintain a balance in his town between the forces of good and light and the forces of darkness, as embodied by Mr. Potter. While his heart yearns for pure artistic freedom and expression, it must find that expression in a balanced way.

Our heart energy is the meeting point between the physical and the spiritual worlds. It is not enough to simply *have* pure joy and spirit — those qualities must be

91

integrated with action for the greater good. Often the desires of the heart must become servants of a higher calling. So it is with this classic holiday film.

When our heart functions well, our outlook on life is cheerful and upbeat, our sleep is restful, and our blood circulation is good. When our heart is disharmonious, our prevalent emotion is anxiety. It's hard to see the bigger picture, our sleep is disturbed, we may have palpitations, and our thoughts are not clear. Excessive stress, overwork, lack of sleep, drinking to the point of intoxication, excessive use of drugs (including pharmaceuticals), excessive emotions, trauma, depression or grief, and unhealthy lifestyle imbalances all can damage the heart and inhibit its ability to function. The heart also is susceptible to excessive heat and the consumption of yin and blood. Maintaining the appropriate balance of water and fire is vital to the heart's health.

The heart has an intimate relationship with the kidney system, which corresponds to the element of water. TCM says that the heart gives the kidneys fire to warm up the water, and the kidneys give the heart water to cool off the fire. This symbiotic relationship maintains the balance of appropriate energy within the heart. Life itself consumes both the water energy and the fire energy, but being in harmony with the seasons can help to minimize the early consumption of these precious energies.

It's good to cultivate your heart energy at any time of the year, but during the summer, you'll find the largest amount of natural energy available to calm and nourish your heart and shen.

Tools for Summer

During the summer months, we tend to feel our best. The days are long and warm, and we spend more time outside, exercising and breathing fresh air. Our natural energy is at its peak, and the largest amount of yang energy is available to us, so it's important that our actions support this increased vitality. These include altering our diet, establishing an appropriate herbal program, exercising, and meditation. It's also a good idea to protect our yin by making sure we get enough rest, taking care of our skin, and drinking plenty of water.

It's important to do these things year round, of course, but the strength of the summer sun and the increased time we spend outdoors in this season makes them even more important.

Good rest varies for different individuals. One general guideline is that we should get at least six hours of sleep a night, combined with afternoon naps or rest periods after exercise or outdoor activities.

Taking care of the skin involves using plenty of sun block, even if you have darker skin, and applying a natural moisturizer like aloe vera to your skin after exposure to the sun. You can use aloe vera directly from the plant itself, or in the form of a pure gel or lotion. The skin is the largest organ of the body, so it's especially important to take care of it.

While it's important to drink at least sixty-four ounces of clean water every day throughout the year, it is vital during the summer. Our outdoor activities and increased summer exercise routine consume more water within the body. So it's crucial to replenish that fluid with at least sixty-four ounces of water a day. Juices, teas, smoothies, and other drinks are beneficial, but they do not serve as substitutes for water.

The summer is an enjoyable time of year for most people. Because the days are longer, we should take the opportunity to spend time outside, watching the sun set, breathing fresh air, and enjoying the beauty of the natural world. Summer is a good time to become involved in creative projects — taking an art class, designing a garden, writing poetry, doing chi kung or yoga, or just writing in your journal. Whatever you feel drawn to do, do it!

Case Study: Chronic Fatigue

Jim, age fifty-two, came to see me after having worked with several other talented, holistic health practitioners. He had been battling chronic fatigue for years and, while the work he had done with other practitioners had been helpful, he still found himself exhausted. We discussed the basic concepts of Chinese medicine and my particular way of working with them. We talked about the seasons and the ways we can use the different energies available in each period to strengthen and harmonize our energy. We also talked about Jim's emotional state. He shared his feelings of isolation and loneliness, and said he had felt this way for most of his life. I suggested there was a probable connection between his emotional state and his health. He acknowledged this and expressed his fear that the pattern was so deeply engrained, he didn't know if it could be changed. But he said he was willing to try.

We began working in the middle of summer, so I explained to Jim the basics of harmonizing with the energy of summer. During the summer, it is possible to build the traits of being open, friendly and sharing. Jim already ate a clean and healthy diet, so there was little to change there. I suggested that he begin taking my herbal formulas "Nourishment" (see page 119) and "Freedom" (see page 99). "Nourishment" is designed to strengthen the digestive system while building a sense of center and balance. "Freedom" helps one to harmonize with the energy of summer, to become more open and alive. I suggested that Jim make continuing efforts to be more social — that he say "Hi" to people he encountered and begin to engage people socially whenever he could. He was too tired for strenuous exercise, he said, so I taught him the chi kung exercises for summer. I also gave him an acupuncture treatment to harmonize his energy with the summer.

The next week when I saw Jim, he felt basically the same. He liked the herbal formulas I had given him, but his tiredness made it difficult to practice the chi kung exercises. The biggest improvement he noticed was in his state of mind. He attributed this to his reaching out to others and engaging them socially. Even though he felt awkward doing it, afterward he always felt lighter and more alive. I gave Jim another treatment to harmonize him with the summer.

Because of Jim's financial limitations, I didn't see him very often. He came to see me when the seasons began to change and for another session during that three-month period. Each time we discussed the basic principles of the coming season, including how his diet should change. I gave him the appropriate herbal formulas and taught him the chi kung exercises for each season. He could see that the work we were doing was helpful. Each time I saw Jim he was a little better. He continued to make small, yet consistent steps toward wellness.

Diet

In summer, as our natural energy reaches its peak, the optimal diet is one of replenishment. The summer diet is similar to the spring diet, including higher proportions of lighter foods and emphasizing vegetables, especially leafy green vegetables (both steamed and raw), light soups, and fish. However, in the summer diet it is less important to cleanse and more important to replenish the body with vitamins, minerals, and fluids lost because of increased temperature and activity levels. We do this by increasing the proportion of fruits we eat while emphasizing the basic principles of the spring diet.

Fruits are one of the great natural resources of summer. Their sweet taste emphasizes the joy of being alive. Increasing the fruits in our diet is an ideal way to harmonize with the energy of summer.

In general, fruits are cooling, moisturizing, and replenishing; they're also high in vitamins, minerals, and natural sugars. If possible, we should eat fruits that have not been sprayed with pesticides, that have ripened on the tree, that are native to the areas in which we live, and that are in season. While it might be difficult to grow enough food for the earth's entire population without pesticides, they are extremely harmful to our bodies and to our environment. It's worth the extra cost to get fruits that are pesticide-free and organically grown.

In today's fast-moving world, allowing fruits to ripen on the tree can be economically prohibitive. The rush to get fruits to market necessitates picking them early and allowing them to ripen while on display. But much of their health benefit is lost that way.

Eating locally grown fruit has many benefits. It has gone through the same seasons you have and adapted to them in similar ways. Also, locally grown fruits stay on the tree longer, with both health and taste benefits.

Eating foods in their natural season is preferable, as they have qualities that help the body to harmonize with that season. For instance, summer fruits are cooling. If they are eaten in winter, their cooling effects will create an imbalance, as an abundance of cool energy is already present in the winter.

While eating a summer diet with a lot of fruit is healthy, it's important not to eat *too many* fruits. Fruits are high in natural sugars and are rich, cooling, and moisturizing. If eaten in excess, they produce too much moisture in the body. In TCM, we call this dampness. Excess dampness has many harmful effects within the body, including decreased energy levels, weakened digestive power, foggy thinking, slowness, sluggish behavior, and lowered immunity. Dampness is caused by many factors, including eating processed sugar, processed foods, and fried foods; excess consumption of cold or cooling substances; and excessive consumption of fruits and fruit juices. One way to minimize dampness is to eat the whole fruit, not just the juice. Fruit juice in small quantities is good for you, but in large quantities it causes dampness. It's hard to give a firm guideline for how much juice is healthy to drink, because each person's body is different. Instead, you should become sensitive to how your body reacts. The natural sugars are more concentrated in juice and can be difficult to digest. If you especially enjoy fruit juice, try diluting it with equal amounts of water. Another way to minimize the damp-producing aspects of fruit is to cook it. When something is cooked, its cooling properties are minimized; it becomes warmer, holds less fluid, and is easier to digest. There are several ways to cook fruit, including baking, steaming, frying (although frying tends to enhance the damp aspects of the fruit), and boiling. Table 8 lists several common fruits and their actions on the body.

Fruit	Properties	Actions
Apricot	Sweet and sour taste, cool temperature	Cooling and moisturizing to the lungs, enhances the yin and the body fluids, and calms the shen; should not be eaten to excess.
Avocado	Sweet taste, cool temperature	Enhances the yin, is moisturizing to the lungs and intestines, and is high in monounsaturated oils; beneficial to nursing mothers
Banana	Sweet taste, cooling temperature	Enhances the yin and is moisturizing to the lungs and intestines.
Cherry	Sweet taste, slightly	Tonifies the chi and the digestion, tonifies the body in general, is moisturizing and nourishing, and rids the body of excess acid.
Fig is	Sweet taste, cool temperature	Moisturizes the lungs and intestines, tonifies the digestion, and extremely alkalizing.
Grape	Sweet and sour taste, cool temperature	Moisturizes the body, tonifies the chi and blood, and strengthens the liver and kidneys.
Grapefruit	Sweet and sour taste, cool temperature	Strengthens digestion, moisturizes the body, and is high in vitamin C. Grapefruit seed extract is a natural antibiotic.

Table 8

97

ONE TRIP AROUND THE SUN

Lemon	Sour taste, cool temperature	Strengthens digestion, moves liver chi and chi in general, aids in the breakdown of fat, has powerful antiseptic and anti-microbial activities, and is high in vitamin C.
Mango	Sweet taste, cool temperature	Moisturizes the body and builds the body fluids. In small amounts, tonifies the chi.
Orange & tangerine	Sweet and sour taste, cool temperature	Strengthens digestion, replenishes body fluids, moisturizes the body, and calms the shen. High in vitamin C.
Papaya	Sweet taste, cool temperature	Tonifies the digestion, moisturizes the body, and builds body fluids. Seeds contain the digestive enzyme papin.
Peach	Sweet taste, cool temperature	Moisturizes the body and builds body fluids. Pit is used to remove blood stagnation.
Pear	Sweet taste, cool temperature	Moisturizes the body and lungs, builds body fluids, and calms the shen.
Pineapple	Sweet and sour taste, cool temperature	Strengthens the digestion, replenishes body fluids, and removes excessive damp heat. Contains the digestive enzyme bromelin.
Plum	Sweet taste, cool temperature	Builds body fluids, moisturizes the intestines, and benefits the liver.
Pomegranate	Sweet and sour taste, neutral temperature	Moisturizes the body, benefits the liver and the blood, and cleanses the bladder.
Raspberry	Sweet and sour taste, neutral temperature	Stops fluid loss, benefits and detoxifies the blood, strengthens the liver and kidneys, and harmonizes the menstrual system. The leaf is a widely used Western herb for the female menstrual system.
Strawberry	Sweet and sour taste, cool temperature	Strengthens digestion, moisturizes the lungs, and aids the body fluids. High in vitamin C.
Watermelon	Sweet taste, cool temperature	Extremely moisturizing to the body, removes damp heat through its diuretic actions, benefits the heart and bladder, and calms the shen.

98

The summer diet is a continuation of the spring diet. You should continue eating meals that are light and easy to digest, and avoid heavy meals and foods that are excessively rich and overburdening. Continue eating smaller, more frequent meals and compensate for the lack of food with an increase in your fluid intake. Eating smaller amounts more frequently will allow your system to be more open and free-flowing, and will help to harmonize your body with the open yang energy of summer.

The color associated with the element of fire is red. In Chinese thought, red is the most yang color. It is symbolic of the hot, moving quality of the burning fire. Red foods, some of which are hot and spicy, can stimulate the mind because of their vibrant color. Mixing red vegetables into salads and soups is an excellent way to include them in your diet. It's interesting to note that red chilies and jalapeno peppers are both rich in capsicum. Capsicum is beneficial to the heart, helping to increase cardiac strength and vigor while stimulating blood circulation.

Food preparation methods for summer are similar to those for spring, but summer allows you to include a higher proportion of raw, fresh foods. Raw foods tend to be cool and can be difficult to digest and absorb, but the abundance of natural enzymes in raw food makes the increased demand on the digestive fire worthwhile.

According to TCM, the bitter taste corresponds with summer and the fire element. It is balanced by the salty taste. The bitter taste has the ability to clear heat, cool pathogenic fire, detoxify the liver and the blood, and calm the shen. The salty flavor, which includes minerals such as potassium and calcium, disperses stagnated energy while deeply nourishing and sustaining. In summer, it's good to eat these two tastes in higher proportions.

Listed below are some basic food principles for summer:

1. **Basically the same as spring.** Eat plenty of steamed vegetables and salads, light and refreshing vegetable and fish soups, and your favorite fish dishes.

99

The summer is a great time to grill food. Take advantage of the warm weather and eat outside in the fresh air.

2. **Fruit salads.** Mix your favorite fruits together based on color, action, taste, and nutritional content. Try sprinkling a little rose water on a fruit salad. Rose helps open and balance the heart.

3. **Fruit juices and smoothies.** These make an excellent base for supplements and herbs. Try to use fruits with supplements that have similar actions. Don't overdo the fruit juices and cooling smoothies, though. If you notice your stomach feels a little cold, try drinking some warm ginger tea.

Herbal Formula: "Freedom"

The Nature's Roar™ custom formula "Freedom" is designed to harmonize the heart and promote the graceful opening of the heart and mind. It aids in the process of cultivating the shen and in developing compassion, honesty, and love. It can be taken all year long to enhance the spirit, relax the mind, and help dissolve stress. Or, you can take it from June 21 to September 21 to harmonize your heart with the fullness of summer. This formula contains schizandra, polygala, salvia, longan, reishi, zizyphus, and albizzia flower.

Case Study: Workout

Steve, a tall, thin forty-eight-year-old, had been an athlete all his life. He still competed in triathlons. He came to see me because he had noticed that in the past few years training had become increasingly difficult for him — he didn't seem to have as much energy or drive. His first session with me was in early spring. I explained the basic concepts and principles of seasonal harmony, especially the aspects related to diet and exercise. I recommended he follow the diet and exercise programs laid out in this book. I also had him begin taking herbs. I kept him on my herbal formula "Nourishment" (see page 119) year-round, and added the appropriate formula for the season we were in.

The next week he returned very enthusiastic, having altered his training program to incorporate a lot more stretching. "Shifting the areas of focus with the seasons makes a lot of sense," he said. He made significant changes in his diet to follow my dietary recommendations and continued taking my herbal formulas "Nourishment" and "Rhythm" (see page 80).

Steve came to see me again about a month later. He reported that his energy was better. The change was subtle, but the changes in his diet and exercise were beginning to have an effect. He continued taking the herbs and became aware of their benefits when he was out of town for a week and forgot to bring them along. "Without my herbs, I felt as though I was dragging," he noted.

At the beginning of summer, Steve came in for another session and we discussed the basic concepts of the fire element and modifications of diet and exercise. I recommended that he substitute the summer formula "Freedom" (see page 99) for the spring formula "Rhythm." He reported that he felt much better — his energy was stronger and his training sessions were going well.

Six weeks later, Steve reported that his energy was stronger than it had been in years. At this point I began seeing him about twice every three months. Each time the season changed he came in and we talked about the upcoming season, modified his diet, and adjusted his exercise and herbal programs. He then came in again sometime during the middle of the season, and each time he reported a sense of deep wellness, reporting, "My workouts are as good as they were many years ago."

Exercise

The summer is a time of full yang, and the basic energetic theme of the season is fullness. The optimal kinds of exercise for summer are those that work the body over a sustained period of time, build a vigorous sweat, and increase the body's cardiovascular stamina. In the summer, it's best to exercise in the late morning, preferably outdoors, doing exercises that help the body use all the energy available during the summer, and exercising for lengthy periods.

The heart, which corresponds to the summer, rules the cardiovascular system. Therefore, the summer is an excellent time to use exercise to build endurance. Any form of exercise is fine during the summer; hiking, yoga, martial arts, swimming, running, skating, walking, and biking are all beneficial, if they're performed to emphasize cardiovascular stamina and endurance. The pace is a bit slower, but the duration of the exercise is longer. The focus is on higher repetitions with less weight.

Exercise	Modifications for summer
Hiking	Walk on flatter trails for longer distances.
Marital arts	Concentrate on high repetitions of movements.
Weight lifting	Use more repetitions and less weight.
Running	Run longer distances at slower speeds.

Chi Kung

During the summer, it's best to use chi kung to stretch the chest, open and cultivate the shen, and strengthen the heart. The basic nei kung posture for the summer be-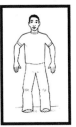gins with the basic posture (See Figure 15). Your arms, however, should be straight out to the sides at shoulder level, palms facing out. Your fingers should point up to the sky and be spread wide to open the palm. Both the heart and pericardium meridians run through the palm. Opening the palm allows the chi in those meridians to flow more effectively. Your joints should not be locked, but open and stretched. Having your arms out at the sides opens the rib cage and creates more space for the heart. Your breathing should be in through the nose and out through the nose, with the tongue touching the roof of your mouth.

Figure 16

Figure 15

103

The chi kung exercise for summer begins in the nei kung posture (see Figure 16). Your arms are out to the sides at shoulder level, palms facing out, fingers pointing up to the sky and spread wide. With the first inhale, move your hands in toward your heart and then down slightly. As your hands near your chest, rotate the palms to almost touch your heart, then expand them out across your chest with a slight upward movement. Your inhale ends with your hands in front of your shoulders and your palms facing your body. Your exhale begins as the palms rotate out and press out, going back to their original starting position. This exercise gathers energy to the heart and chest, so they can expand. After your chest has been expanded with the energy, the breath is released to create openness, prevent stagnation, and bring balance to the heart.

The pace of the exercise is slow and meditative, like most chi kung. Allow yourself to focus specifically on the heart and the heart energy, and do as many repetitions as time allows.

Journaling

The fire element is the most extraverted aspect of the seasonal story. It speaks of the beautiful flowering of consistent growth. Fire energy often ignites creative passions  and offers new ways of looking at things. This next phase of the journaling process involves actively working with this energy; it is common to encounter anxieties, phobias, neuroses, untrue belief systems, and other erratic mental and emotional patterns. As you move through whatever issues need to be expressed, you will begin to uncover feelings like love, compassion, kindness, awareness, honesty, and generosity. At this point, it's common to feel as if everything is changing and you no longer know who you are. You might find it difficult to continue old patterns that served you before. This is natural and normal — just continue with your writing. The process of becoming self-aware is as much about letting go of what no longer serves you as it is about manifesting your true self.

As you feel safe, allow yourself to engage your tendencies to be less than honest with yourself. Begin to compassionately ask what these tendencies are hiding — what you are afraid of revealing. What do you gain by not truthfully accepting yourself? What is it you need to express your true self? What are the issues you associate with being truthful?

Remember, the process of transformation can be difficult, even traumatic. Be gentle with yourself. There's no need to push, pry, or force yourself to open. This is an organic process; it will unfold when it's ready, and not before. Ask yourself these questions whenever you feel the time is appropriate.

Meditation

Summer mediation is best done in a posture such as lotus or half-lotus, sitting in a chair, or sitting on the knees, but it can be done standing or walking. Your hands are in prayer pose —palms pressed together, thumbs resting in the space above the abdomen but below the sternum, shoulders relaxed, and elbows out to the sides. The meditation for summer uses the basic breath: Inhale through your nose, exhale through your nose, with your tongue touching the roof of your mouth. Your eyes should be opened ten percent, and your mind focused on your heart energy. The goal of the meditation is to allow your heart to open slowly and gently, as a flower would blossom. No urgency or force is applied. Rather, your focus is on creating a neutral, honest, and safe space for the heart's natural process. Another valuable form of the meditation is contemplating concepts like *"Compassion is . . ." "Generosity is . . ." "Kindness is . . ."* and *"Love is . . ."* The meditation for summer is a process of contacting the shen. The shen extends from a point in the center top of your head to your heart.

Allow this beautiful energy to awaken and move down from the top of your head to your heart.

This is a gentle process, so be patient with yourself. You may want to keep your journal close by to write down any thoughts, feelings, or inspirations you discover. Practice for as long as time permits.

Chapter 7

Earth

 THE EARTH PHASE is the energy of balance, harmony, and stability. Within the five elements, earth represents the time when the seasons are changing. Activated during the equinoxes and solstices, earth's grounding and harmonizing influence helps in the transition of energy from one level to the next. Earth energy provides a balanced, stable bridge between the season that is ending and the one beginning. Seasonally, the earth is connected to the end of summer, which is often referred is to as Indian or late summer.

The Stomach and Spleen

The organ systems related to earth energy are the spleen system, which includes the pancreas (yin), and the stomach (yang). The stomach and spleen have several important functions: They govern the digestive process, eating, the appetite, the muscles, the flesh, and the limbs. Both are involved in the production of blood. The stomach and spleen help to direct the movement of energy. The stomach aids energy in its downward movement, while the spleen helps in its upward course. These two organs also play a vital role in the functioning of the immune system. Within the body, the earth energy is the ability to be calm and patient while moving through the ever-changing aspects of life.

The stomach and spleen are the two main digestive organs, although the small intestine absorbs nutrients and is important in the process as well. From a TCM perspective, the stomach receives the food, grinds it up, and sends the pure essence to the spleen. The spleen first absorbs the pure nutritive aspects of the food, then transforms that substance into a precursor that will become chi and blood. The spleen also is responsible for transporting the absorbed nutrition to various organs in the body. The spleen is called the *foundation of postnatal chi* because it is responsible for continually creating the chi we use in our daily lives. This is in contrast to the *prenatal chi*, also known as *jing*, which comes from the parents at the time of conception and is a predetermined amount of life energy. The spleen's ability to produce postnatal chi partly determines our relative vitality on a day-to-day basis. When your stomach and spleen are functioning well, your digestive processes will be smooth and effective, your body will have an abundance of chi and blood, and your various body parts will receive ample nourishment. When your stomach and spleen are not functioning well, your digestive process will be unsettled and lack effectiveness. Your body may have difficulty absorbing adequate nutrition, and you may suffer from a deficiency of either chi or blood, or both. The body may lack the basic amount of energy needed for daily activities, and various organs may not receive enough nourishment. The ability to produce enough chi on a daily basis is crucial to your general health and well-being.

108

Earth energy is known as the *digestive fire*. It works in cooperation with the kidney energy to power our digestive ability. Every time something enters the body, the digestive flame has to "heat" it up to body temperature so it can be digested. Warming up cold foods requires a lot of energy, whereas warm soups, teas, and cooked foods enhance the effectiveness of the flame. Cold drinks, ice cream, smoothies, and raw foods, on the other hand, impair the digestive flame. If you learn only one thing from this book, let it be this: **To enhance and preserve your vitality, be sure to eat or drink something warm after eating something cold.** It's fine to eat ice cream. In fact, it's one of the sweetest treats. But cold foods and drinks must be balanced by warming foods or drinks. In the warmer months, it's okay to be a bit more lenient with this policy. In the colder months, however, it's essential to prevent cold foods from smothering the digestive flame. Guarding and protecting the flame will go a long away toward ensuring the health, well-being, and vitality of your body.

The stomach and spleen systems rule eating and the appetite. When these systems are functioning well, you have a healthy appetite and balanced eating habits, and your body is less prone to allergies and food sensitivities. When the stomach and spleen are not functioning well, your appetite may be poor or erratic, your eating habits and dietary patterns may be unhealthy or dysfunctional, and you may have allergies and sensitivities to various types of food.

The spleen's nourishing capabilities keep the flesh healthy and in proper working order. When the spleen is functioning well, muscles are full, flesh is vigorous, blood is abundant, and the limbs are in harmony with the rest of the body. When the spleen is not functioning well, muscles are weak or underdeveloped, flesh may be unhealthy and slow to heal, blood may be deficient, and the limbs may not be in optimal condition.

As I mentioned earlier, the stomach rules descending and the spleen rules ascending. One of the ways earth energy works within the body is by balancing these two opposing forces. The stomach energy, when functioning well, rules the proper downward flow of energy within the body. In charge of moving food down through

109

the gastrointestinal tract, it also helps move chi downward through the meridians or in any other part of the body. The spleen, which is in charge of ascending energy, maintains the organs in their proper upright alignment and prevents them from sinking into prolapse. It also maintains the proper posture in the body by regulating the musculature and providing the necessary upward-moving energy. When the stomach and spleen are functioning well, there is a natural balance within the body. Energies or substances that need to move upward or downward have the energy to do so. When the stomach and spleen are not functioning well, you might experience acid reflux, hiccoughs, vomiting, prolapsed organs, hemorrhoids, poor posture, diarrhea, and general imbalance.

The stomach and spleen play an important role in the proper functioning of the immune system. The spleen provides the precursor to what eventually becomes *wei*, or defensive chi. From the TCM perspective, the health of the wei chi partly ensures the first line of defense in the immune system. On a deeper level, it is the balancing energy of the spleen and stomach that helps to govern the immune system and prevent autoimmune responses.

Positive emotions associated with earth energy include balance, healthy self-esteem, confidence, stability, patience, consistency, and dependability. When the stomach and spleen are functioning well, your outlook will be grounded, balanced, and confident. Negative emotions of the earth energy system include worry, excessive ego, low self-esteem, impatience, and a lack of confidence, dependability, and consistency. When the stomach and spleen organ systems are not functioning well, people often are unable to conduct their lives in a grounded and integrated fashion.

Note that *self-esteem* and *ego* are not the same. Self-esteem is a healthy view of yourself that does not depend on what others think, say, or feel about you: It comes from within. Ego, on the other hand, comes from the outside and is based on the approval of others. It has little to do with how you view yourself. From an ego point of view, you do things in order to gain acceptance from others. This often leads to unhealthy feelings about yourself. Because your opinion of yourself is based on things that are external to yourself, the ego constantly needs approval from others. If that approval diminishes or disappears altogether, the ego suffers terribly. But the ego is not the true self.

When your spleen and stomach are strong, your body functions in a balanced and effective manner. Food is digested smoothly, and your body makes an abundance of chi and blood. Your emotions are grounded, and you can make decisions with patience and stability. When the spleen and stomach are weakened, your body struggles. Your digestive process becomes unbalanced, you experience a deficiency of chi and blood, and your body lacks energy. It's difficult to stay grounded, and you tend to overreact to things.

The stomach and spleen are particularly susceptible to climatic disorders of dampness and excessive heat or cold.

Tools for Earth

While it technically happens during the changing of the seasons, the earth phase is present every day. It's present when the sunrise gives birth to a new day and when night begins as the sun sets. Cultivating earth energy every day is important because it is the center from which all the other energies rotate. One of the ways we cultivate earth energy is by not being overly reactive. We must realize that life is continually changing and, while certain experiences may be painful or unpleasant, they will pass. When you understand this, you can discipline yourself not to react wildly to stresses and unpleasant experiences. A famous Taoist story illustrates this point:

> There was once a farmer who had a son. One day the farmer's horse wandered off. The farmer and his son looked for the horse all day and into the night. That evening, when the villagers learned of the farmer's misfortune,

111

they all said how unlucky he was to have lost his horse. The farmer simply said "maybe." The next morning the horse returned, and it brought several other fine horses with it. That night when the villagers heard of the farmer's good fortune, they all said how lucky he was. The farmer simply replied "maybe." The next day, the farmer's son broke his arm while trying to ride one of the new horses. That night when the villagers heard of the farmer's bad fortune, they all said how unlucky he was. The farmer simply said "maybe." The next morning, imperial troops came through the village enlisting all of the eligible young men to go off to battle. The soldiers took all of the village's young men, with the exception of the farmer's son, due to his broken arm. That night when the villagers heard of the farmer's good fortune, they all said how lucky he was. The farmer simply said "maybe."

This story beautifully illustrates the power of avoiding reactivity. As we learn to avoid overreacting to the dramas of life, our bodies and minds become more stable and centered. This is one of the main ways we can cultivate the power of earth energy within.

Case Study: Earth

Stephanie, now twenty-two, had been a successful model since the age of eighteen.

She was tall, thin, and beautiful. She also had an eating disorder and had been in therapy for years, trying to work out the underlying issues that caused her bulimia. She came to see me to get some extra support.

During her first visit, we talked about her relationships with her family. A difficult childhood had left her feeling isolated, with little connection to either her mother or her father. In fact, it was hard for her to feel close to anybody. She reported an overwhelming sense of being too large and taking up too much space, and these feelings seemed to be at the core of her dysfunction.

I spent some time talking with her about earth energy, explaining that healthy self-esteem came from within and had nothing to do with the approval of others. She said she understood, but her feelings were deep and well-entrenched. I taught her the earth meditation and recommended she begin taking my herbal formula "Nourishment" (see page 119). But I avoided discussing diet and exercise, as she already worked out obsessively. Before she left, I gave her an acupuncture treatment to harmonize her earth energy.

The next week, Stephanie reported that she felt basically the same. She liked the herbs because she felt they gave her more energy, but she had not spent much time doing the meditation. When she looked inside, it was too painful to continue. I again gave her a treatment to harmonize her earth energy.

The following week, she told me she felt bettere, and the herbs and the acupuncture seemed to be helping. I talked to her about some of the seasonal concepts. When I mentioned adjusting her exercise routine according to the seasons, she became interested; so we spent some time talking about how to use exercise as a tool to harmonize with the seasons. I gave her another acupuncture treatment to harmonize her earth energy.

When I saw Stephanie a week later, she said she really liked adjusting her exercise program to harmonize with the energy of seasons —this made a lot of sense to her. Her response was important, because it gave us something she felt comfortable talking to me about; it was a big step for her to have that sense of closeness with me. Once again I gave her a treatment to harmonize her earth energy.

I continued seeing Stephanie for many months. She traveled often for her modeling career, but whenever she was in town she came for treatments. Overall, she seemed to get better. She continued taking the herbs and used her exercise program to harmonize with the seasons. But making substantial progress in the emotional arenas was difficult for her, although she did report that working with me had helped her develop a little more closeness with her family. Our work together help her body stay healthy and helped her to take small but consistent steps toward a sense of wholeness and emotional well-being. I am continuing to work with Stephanie.

Diet

The earth diet is a constant throughout the year. Because of its balancing aspect, it 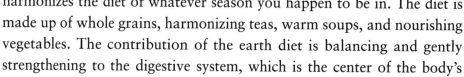 harmonizes the diet of whatever season you happen to be in. The diet is made up of whole grains, harmonizing teas, warm soups, and nourishing vegetables. The contribution of the earth diet is balancing and gently strengthening to the digestive system, which is the center of the body's vitality and well-being.

Whole grains are related to earth energy. Although knowledge of grains and their incorporation into the Western diet has been mostly forgotten, whole grains provide the body with high levels of protein and amino acids, whole-spectrum balanced nutrients, fiber, and calcium. In the latest dietary lingo, they are called *complex carbohydrates*, and rightly so. More difficult to digest, the whole grain requires plenty of chewing to sufficiently coat the bolus. It also needs proper preparation. Although whole grains take a bit more effort to cook and consume, their health benefits are worth the trouble. They provide the body with a consistent and stable energy source and help balance, strengthen, and steady the digestion and metabolism. They also gently soothe the emotions, calm the mind, and help us maintain a healthy elimination system.

According to TCM, whole grains balance and tone the earth energy. It's wise to eat a wide variety of whole grains, because each has a different set of actions and properties. Whole grains are neutral in temperature and have a variety of tastes. They dry dampness and bring fertility to the "soil"— ancient Chinese medical texts are filled with associations between the body and farming, the body and social order. The metaphor of the soil becoming fertile through the consistent consumption of grains means that the grains help the digestive organs operate under optimal conditions.

Because grains can be difficult to digest, it is important to prepare them correctly. Prewashing and scrubbing removes dirt, indigestible fiber, and other particles, making the grains easier to break down. Presoaking initiates the sprouting process, which makes grains more digestible, improves their flavor, and activates latent enzymes and nutrients. While presoaking is not necessary, it is recommended. There are differing opinions as to the best use of the soaking water. Some assert that it contains many beneficial nutrients and energies and so should be consumed. Others believe the soaking water contains the waste products from the sprouting process and should be discarded. Try both approaches and let your own experience guide your decision. To soak grains, simply add water to the grains and let the mixture sit for eight to twelve hours. Be sure to use clean water.

It's important to cook grains thoroughly. Add water, the grains, and mineral-rich sea salt to your pot. The general rule of thumb is two cups of water for every one cup of grain (one cup of grain feeds two people). Bring the water to a boil, then turn the flame to low and allow the grains to simmer for thirty to forty minutes. Make sure they are well cooked before you eat them. Usually they are ready when all the water is gone. The mineral-rich sea salt tenderizes the grain, making it more digestible. Vary the amount of salt based on the season. When it's closer to winter, use more salt (a quarter-teaspoon per cup of grain); when closer to summer, use less (an eighth-teaspoon per cup).

Use a heavy pot to cook grain (such as an enamel-lined cast iron pot with a heavy lid). The heavy pot makes the grain more flavorful, helps keep chi from dispersing, and makes the grain more digestible and toning. You also can prepare grains in a pressure cooker, which is especially effective in colder weather. A crock pot is also good for this kind of deep cooking.

Grains are especially tasty when roasted; the roasting increases their warming

115

effect and aids in digestion. Roasted grains are especially helpful in colder weather and when the body has diarrhea. Roast grains in a pot or pan over a medium flame, stirring continuously. Continue until the grain is golden brown and aromatic.

Another popular way to prepare grains is in porridge, or *congee*. Porridge is a thick stew similar to oatmeal that's often eaten for breakfast. Congee is a combination of white rice and Chinese herbs. It's commonly prepared for the deficient or debilitated, but anyone who wants to improve their earth energy will benefit from it. Congee is made by mixing six parts of water to one part grain, then cooking the mixture slowly for a long period of time (two to three hours) over a low flame. White rice is commonly used, because it's the easiest to digest, but any grain is fine. Herbs that tone the digestion and strengthen the chi are used in the mixture, including some variety of ginseng (American ginseng, white ginseng, or red ginseng), astragalus, fresh ginger, dried ginger, poria, codonopsis, and licorice. You can brew the herbs and use the tea to cook the grains, or simply add the herbs when you're cooking the grains. Either cooking method is effective. Refrigerate the leftover grains and use them within two days. Table 9 (see page 116) lists several grains and their actions on the body.

The earth diet, eaten all year long, is the foundation of the whole diet. It is made up of the basic nourishing aspects that support and balance the system throughout the changing seasons. The earth components and principles within the diet stay basically the same all year.

Foundations of the earth diet include warming soups and teas. Warming soup can be anything from a warm vegetable broth to an exotic stew. As long as it is warm in temperature and relatively easy to digest, it qualifies. Warming soups can be eaten before the main course to enliven the digestive energy or serve as the main course. They aid the digestive flame and are generally nourishing to the whole body. On cold days, they can profoundly warm the body. Warming teas are similar to warming soups. As long as they are warm in temperature and not filled with milk and sugar,

116

Grain	Properties	Actions
Amaranth	Bitter and sweet taste, cool temperature	Dries dampness and strengthens the lungs and the spleen.
Barley	Sweet and salty taste, cool temperature	Strengthens the spleen and stomach; builds blood, yin, and fluids; and calms nerves. Mildly laxative and easier to digest then many grains. Clears dampness by promoting diuresis. Whole barley is preferred, as it is more nutritious. Pan roast for the treatment of diarrhea
Buckwheat	Sweet taste, neutral temperature	Gently cleanses and tonifies the intestines, strengthens blood vessels, lowers blood pressure, and is said to serve as an antidote to radiation. Pan roast to treat diarrhea.
Millet while	Sweet and salty taste, cool temperature	Tonifies the spleen, stomach, and kidneys; drains dampness building yin and moistening dryness. Has anti-fungal properties and is effective when treating candida disharmonies.
Oats	Sweet and bitter taste, warm temperature	Strengthens stomach and spleen, calms the shen, tonifies and harmonizes chi, strengthens the bones and connective tissue, and calms the gastrointestinal tract.
Quinoa	Sweet and sour taste, warm temperature	Extremely toning to the whole system, high in nutrient content, and generally strengthening.
Rice	Sweet taste, neutral temperature	Tonifies the spleen and stomach, tonifies the chi, aids in the elimination process, calms the shen. Brown rice is more toning than white rice.
Rye	Bitter taste, neutral temperature	Tonifies the spleen, moves and harmonizes the liver chi, drains dampness, and tonifies the flesh.
Wheat	Sweet and salty taste, cool temperature	Tonifies the heart and kidneys, calms the shen, builds moisture, and builds flesh. Many people are allergic to wheat, so it must tried with some caution.

Table 9

Type of tea	Properties	Actions
Green tea	Bitter taste, cool temperature	Cools and calms the liver, moves liver chi, and soothes the shen.
Jasmine tea	Bitter taste, warm temperature	Warms the digestive system and helps break down fatty foods.
Chamomile tea	Bitter taste, cool temperature	Calms and relaxes the body, soothes the liver, and harmonizes the shen.
Citrus tea	Bitter and pungent taste, warm temperature	Harmonizes the stomach and spleen, warms the digestive system, and moves stagnant chi.
Mint tea	Pungent taste, cool temperature	Moves liver chi, cools the stomach, and releases wind heat.
Black tea	Bitter taste, warm temperature	Warms the digestive system and harmonizes the stomach.

Table 10

they are acceptable. There are a plethora of teas to choose from, as seen in Table 10.

The color associated with the element of earth is yellow. In Chinese thought, yellow is symbolic of nourishment and the soil. Yellow foods such as grains and root vegetables help to build chi and center the mind.

The optimal method for preparing earth energy food is smooth and consistent cooking. Cook these foods over a low to medium flame for a medium amount of time. The idea is to create balanced meals. We do this by avoiding extreme cooking methods. It's a good idea to prepare warming and nourishing foods when you're trying to harmonize with earth energy.

According to TCM, the sweet taste corresponds to late summer and the earth element. Sweetness is said to be in the center of all the tastes. It is both mildly toning and gently cleansing. Remember, however, that what the Chinese call the sweet taste is not the ultra-sweet refined sugar taste to which we in the West are accustomed. Rather, it's the sweetness found in the sweet potato. In order to appreciate the sweetness of the earth, you may have to retrain your taste buds.

Another important topic is the consumption of eggs, milk, and cheese in the Western diet. All of these foods are very rich; if eaten excessively, they can cause dampness, phlegm, or stagnation in the earth energy. If eaten within balance, they can nourish the yin. It's difficult to give guidelines as to how much is acceptable, as every body is different. Allow your own experience to guide you.

Listed blow are some basic food principles for earth energy

1. **Plenty of whole grains.** Eat them mixed together, as each has different strengths and weaknesses. Try different cooking methods. Congee, pressure cookers, and crock pots are all good ways to prepare grains.

2. **Fresh vegetables.** Vegetables that are cooked or steamed make up an essential aspect of the earth diet. Eat fresh vegetables at least once a day, if not more often.

3. **Warming and balancing teas.** The digestive organs prefer to be warm. Therefore, it's important throughout the year to drink teas that will regulate, warm, and strengthen the digestive fire. Consistent drinking of any kind of tea, including ginger and chamomile, is a great way to begin warming the digestive flame.

4. **Warming and balancing soups.** Start each meal with a light warming soup, such as miso, vegetable, or chicken. Drinking soups prior to eating gets the digestive organs ready for the food to come. It's an excellent practice, one that will bring health and well-being with consistency.

Herbal Formula: "Nourishment"

The Nature's Roar™ custom formula "Nourishment" harmonizes the spleen and stomach and helps the digestive system to be consistent, stable, and steady. It aids in the process of building healthy self-esteem and confidence. Designed to enhance patience, determination, and persistence, it can be taken all year long to build the power of the digestive system, strengthen chi, and continually balance the earth energy. It contains ginseng (Chinese red and American), codonopsis, poria, atractylodes, licorice, fresh ginger, and jujubee dates.

Case Study: Earth Water

Jim, age thirty-three, is a successful executive in the entertainment industry. After several years in the fast lane, he developed a noncancerous brain tumor that began disrupting his speech, health, and ability to move. He underwent radiation treatment to shrink the tumor. After the radiation was completed, he began seeing me.

Earth energy rules the digestion, muscles, and basic stability of the body, so my first treatment goal was to get his earth energy functioning. I recommended that he eat three to five small meals throughout the day, as opposed to fewer large meals. I also suggested he consume fish two or three times a day. Fish is light and easy to digest, and it is rich in protein.

I recommended he begin taking my herbal formulas "Nourishment" and "Creation" (see page 150) to strengthen both the earth energy and the water energy. After a major debilitating disease, it's often necessary to rebuild the body's core energies. Jim also was working with a physical therapist to regain control of his muscular system and return tone to it. I began giving him acupuncture treatments to open and tone the earth energy.

The next week when I saw him, he reported feeling a little better and a little

120

stronger, but he was still shaky and needed a cane to walk. Some of the numbness was fading, and he was picking up speed in his healing process. He continued taking the two formulas I had recommended.

The next week he reported the same positive trend. He was now taking small walks without the cane. The week after that brought more progress. He had traveled to New York over the weekend, and even after a transcontinental flight and the time change, he reported feeling all right.

He reported the following week that he was taking fairly long walks without the cane. He was still a bit shaky, but definitely improving.

Jim's process continued this way for many weeks. Each week he reported getting better in small increments, which is often the way healing works, especially after major illnesses. Earth energy is slow and steady, and the process works, but you must be persistent and consistent. Jim is still on a steady path toward recovery.

Exercise

The earth energy is related to balance and harmony. The best kinds of exercise to do during the earth phase are those that work to bring all the aspects of the body together. Running, hiking, swimming, yoga, chi kung, martial arts, and weight lifting are all excellent, so long as you practice to a level at which you are tired but not exhausted.

Exercise	Modifications for the Earth Energy
Hiking	Balance between grade of trails and length of distance.
Martial arts	Concentrate on balance.
Weight lifting	Do a medium number of repetitions using medium weights.
Running	Run medium distances at medium speeds.

Chi Kung

During the earth phase it's best to use chi kung to balance and stabilize the body and to harmonize and strengthen the digestive system. The basic nei kung posture for the earth phase begins with the basic posture (see Figure 17). Your arms, however, should be rounded at the level of your solar plexus (above your navel, but below your sternum), with the palms facing your abdomen. The emphasis of the exercise is being grounded in your legs and feet while breathing with your abdomen. The idea is to connect the abdomen to the strength and stability of your legs. The breathing is done in through the nose and out through the nose, with the tongue touching the roof of the mouth.

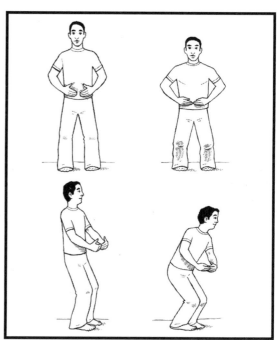

Figure 18

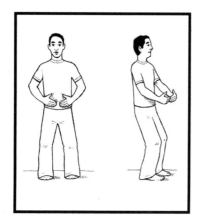

Figure 17

The chi kung exercise for earth energy begins in the earth nei kung posture (see Figure 18, page 122). With the first exhale, bend your knees as if squatting down, but keep your arms rounded and at the level of your solar plexus, with the palms facing the body. Be sure to keep your head up and your back straight as you go down. Once you get as far down as you can comfortably go, take a full breathing cycle (inhale and exhale) while holding the position. As the next inhale begins, return to the starting position, keeping your head up and your back straight. Back at the beginning position, take a full breathing cycle (exhale and inhale) while holding the position. With the next exhale continue the exercise. Do as many repetitions as you can comfortably do.

The pace for this exercise is slow and steady. It is designed to strengthen the legs and the abdominal organs while developing a dependable, consistent rhythm.

Journaling

The earth element, the midpoint of the seasonal story, speaks of being grounded and rooted like an oak tree. In the earth phases it's common to encounter feelings of low  self-worth, lack of confidence, and not knowing who you are or what you want. As you express the patterns that have been stored, you'll begin to uncover feelings of healthy self-esteem, confidence, and a clearer sense of who you are and what you want. A portion of the earth phase is present during each of the other phases. It's the aspect of the cycle that brings the work you are doing to a place of integration and application and often gives you a better perspective of the big picture. Earth energy helps keep you within areas you are ready to deal with and guide you in making practical use of the insights you gain. Learn to trust the earth — it is one of the best supports we have.

Allow yourself to examine who you are. Ask yourself what you value, what is important to you. Then begin to move a little deeper. Ask yourself who you are, how you define yourself. Where or how did you acquire the belief systems you're using to view yourself? Are those systems working for you? Realize that the way we view ourselves and what is important arises from multiple causes. Are the beliefs you use to view yourself working for you? If the answer is yes, fine; if it's no, begin observing the beliefs that aren't working. Allow yourself to honestly express old belief systems and, as you do, allow yourself to change portions of the beliefs to better suit yourself.

We have the power to change the way we measure ourselves. When we do that, we can also change the way we feel about ourselves. Often, we set standards for ourselves that are difficult or even impossible to meet. This invariably brings a feeling of failure and lowers our sense of self-worth. By allowing yourself to truly observe and express the way you measure yourself and allowing yourself to modify the measurements that aren't working for you, you can create a healthier and happier self-image.

Meditation

The meditation for earth energy can be done in a lotus or half-lotus posture, in a seated posture, sitting on the knees, or while walking. The focus of the meditation is on the abdomen, navel, and solar plexus. Your eyes are closed and you breathe in through the nose and out through the nose, with your tongue touching the roof of your mouth. Allow your breath and your mind to focus within the center of the body on your true self. Allow any thoughts, feelings, or emotions that may be triggered to be present. Simply observe the inside of your body with honesty and compassion. As each breath enters your body, feel as if a warm, yellow light is cleansing and healing your abdominal area. The goal of this meditation is to enhance the health, well-being, and harmony of your digestive organs while developing self-esteem. Allow yourself to comfortably relate to any emotions you may need to release. It's a good idea to have a journal nearby and to write down what you feel. With time and practice, you may find both your digestion and your view of yourself improving. Practice for as long as time permits.

Chapter 8

Autumn

AUTUMN IS THE time of decline and of using the things we have worked for, the time of harvest and reaping the benefits after the long summer. It is symbolic of aging, which we see in the leaves as they change colors and fall from the trees. Within the five phases, autumn corresponds to the energy of metal, which is symbolic of the axe that cuts down the plant in order to harvest its fruit.

In general, autumn is the time when the natural energy begins to decline, moving inward and downward. As the weather becomes colder and the days grow shorter, we respond by wearing warmer clothes, drinking warm beverages, and spending more time indoors. We become more introspective and begin the process of storing what we will need to survive the coming winter.

The Lungs, the Large Intestine, and the Metal Element

According to TCM, the organ systems most related to autumn and the metal element are the lungs (yin), and the large intestine (yang). The lung system is considered the most superficial, because of its close relationship and relative proximity to the outer world. The lungs and their main function, breathing, play an important role in the quality and quantity of our day-to-day energy. This is one reason the ancient Chinese masters placed such emphasis on the daily practice of arts that involve deep breathing.

By altering the way we breathe, we can control how we react to any given situation. When we consciously breathe, we use our minds to control our breath and take responsibility for ourselves and our actions. Pause for a moment and take some slow, deep breaths. Notice how your heart rate slows, your thoughts become clearer, and your body relaxes. When our lungs are functioning well and we use our breath consciously, not only do our bodies relax and our minds clear, our emotions also flow smoothly. When our lungs are not functioning well or we are not breathing consciously, our bodies tend to be tense, our minds race, and our emotions are reactive and wild.

The lungs and the large intestine rule the ability to let go. When the lungs release a large breath, the body is able to let go. Similarly, a large bowel movement releases waste products, stimulates movement in the gastrointestinal tract, and has a relaxing effect on the body. When the body lets go of the byproducts of respiration or the waste products from the digestive process, it's ready to receive a fresh inflow of energy. Human beings are ultra-sensitive recording instruments, and every life experience we record must be processed. One of the ways we process the emotional experiences of life is by letting go. The full cycle involves letting experiences come in, learning and growing from them, and then letting them go. Often, these life experiences are painful, and there are times when it's difficult to let go of something or someone. Grieving is the experience of actively feeling all of the pain, hurt, heartache, rejection, and fear connected to life. Crying is one of the ways we actively grieve and let go. The only way to make room for something new to come into the lungs or the large intestine — or into our life, for that matter — is to let go of the old emotions that may be stuck within the body. If the lungs or large intestine are not functioning well, or if some other part of us is unable to let go of a certain experience or emotion, grief and depression settle into the body. When the lungs and large intestine are functioning well and are not obstructed by other parts of our psyche, the experience of life comes in to us fully, and we are able to be process, experience, and let go of it without attachment.

The lungs control our breath, and through that function they control our chi. Part of our daily energy comes from the air we breathe. According to the understanding of physiology within Chinese medicine, a portion of the air we breathe mixes with a portion of the energy we derive from digesting food. These two energies combine to form our daily chi. But the lungs do more than simply manufacture energy. The way they breathe determines the quality of our chi. In TCM, the chi has a distinct characteristic or flavor. If the breath comes into the body in short, erratic bursts, the chi will be less vital and somewhat tense; it will not flow as well. But if the breath comes into the body in long, deep, slow, and rhythmic breaths, the chi will be vigorous and tranquil, and it will flow smoothly throughout the body.

The lung system rules the sinuses, the lungs themselves, the voice, and the entire respiratory tract. When our lungs are clear and strong, our sinuses will be clear, our voice will be strong, and our breathing will be deep and unrestricted. When our lungs are weakened or restricted, our sinuses may be congested, our voice weak, and our breathing shallow and restricted.

Our lungs also play an important role in the first phase of our immune response. Within TCM the lungs, with the help of the spleen, are said to produce and control the *wei*, or defensive, chi. The wei chi circulates at the boundaries of the body and guards it from the harmful effects of pathogens and climatic changes. When our lungs — and, by extension, our wei chi — are strong, our bodies can resist colds and flu. When our lungs and wei chi are weakened, our bodies are prone to catching colds and flu.

The lungs control the opening and closing of the pores, and skin can be thought of as an extension of the lungs. Lungs and skin are made up of similar cells, and both take an active role in respiratory functions. When the lungs are functioning well, they can open and close the pores and allow the skin to breathe effectively. When the lungs are not functioning well, the body is subject to feelings of excessive heat or cold, the mechanism of sweating may be disturbed, and the skin has a hard time performing its respiratory duties.

The large intestine system is responsible for taking the remnants of the digestive process, extracting whatever beneficial fluids remain there, forming feces, and excreting the waste. When the large intestine is not functioning well, we may experience abdominal pain or discomfort, constipation, diarrhea, gas, or general digestive disharmony. When the large intestine is functioning well, our bowels move regularly and without discomfort, our stools are well formed, and our digestive process is smooth.

Positive emotions associated with the lungs include the ability to learn from experiences and then let them go. Negative emotions include melancholy, depression, stored grief, repeating the same mistakes over and over, and the inability to move on.

The lungs are susceptible to atmospheric and climatic influences known within Chinese medicine as wind. They also are averse to conditions of excessive dampness or dryness. The lungs like to be moist and fresh. When there is too much or too little fluid, the lungs function poorly. Obviously, smoking and breathing noxious fumes

129

damage the lungs. The harmful effects of excessive living mentioned in previous chapters also negatively affect the lungs.

Tools for Autumn

A story about two monks clearly illustrates the concept of attachment and release:

> Shiko and Koji were returning home to the monastery after a long journey to one of their patrons when they encountered a beautiful woman who was blocked by a large puddle of mud in the road. Shiko immediately approached the woman and helped her over the puddle.
>
> Several hours later, Koji said, "Shiko, how could you have touched that woman? You know that we are monks, and are thus barred from intimate contact with women!"
>
> Koji replied, "Yes, you are right, Shiko. But who is still carrying her?"

In the story, Koji clearly moves outside of the boundaries by which he lives, but he is able to allow the experience to pass without becoming attached to it. Meanwhile, Shiko has been turning the incident over and over in his mind, waiting for the right time to talk about it. Through finally expressing his preoccupation to Koji, Shiko is able to release whatever attachments he had developed from the experience.

The story is designed to teach us not to get hung up on the experiences of life but simply to let them pass. Koji was able to let whatever feelings he had during the incident pass without thinking about them over and over again and becoming unbalanced by them. This is not, of course, a license to do things we know are wrong or hurtful to others; it's simply an understanding that it is better to stay in the present moment and not dwell on the past or become overly concerned with the future.

During the autumn months, our natural energy begins to move downward and inward. As the days become shorter and the weather becomes cooler, it's wise to begin letting go of what is no longer useful and consolidate what is necessary for the coming winter. We see it in the way animals collect the food they will need to see them through the cold season. We also see it in the way the wheat is separated from the chaff at harvest time. Autumn is a time to focus on our life goals and let go of activities that do not help us reach those goals.

Case Study: Lung Liver

Dennis came to see me after his wife passed away. He was forty-five, and his wife had been forty. They had been happily married for fifteen years when she was diagnosed with breast cancer. The first time I saw Dennis, he was still in a state of shock. It was as if his body was present, but his mental and emotional faculties were elsewhere. As we talked I could see that he was just barely hanging on.

"My wife was the center of my world. I don't know what I'm going to do without her," he said.

I recommended that he join a grief support group, so he would have help expressing and dealing with the pain he was feeling. I also suggested that he begin exercising as much as possible and that he do a lot of journaling, because it's crucial to give our emotions as many pathways for expression as possible to keep them from becoming stuck.

I suggested that Dennis take my herbal formulas "Expression" (see page 134) and "Rhythm" (see page 80). "Expression" would help keep his lung chi flowing so that his breathing would be easier, and "Rhythm" would help keep the chi in the rest of his body flowing smoothly. Both formulas would aid in keeping his chi and emotions moving. This movement is vital, because only when the emotions are moving can they be processed and released. As soon as the emotions become stagnant, they crystallize in the body as deeply held patterns that can be extremely difficult to overcome. I also gave Dennis an acupuncture treatment to open his lungs and soothe his chi.

When I saw Dennis again the next week, he had not done much to help himself. He had yet to call the grief support group, and he had done no journaling, although he had taken the herbs a couple of times. He said he just didn't know how he could go on without his wife. During the whole session, he just sat with me and cried.

The following week, however, he was a little better. He had called the grief support group and had gone to one meeting. He said it was extremely helpful and thanked me for the suggestion. He had taken the herbs every day and thought they were helping. He had not done much journaling yet, but said he thought it would be helpful. And he had started exercising.

The next week, Dennis seemed better. The support group had had a profound effect on him — just being with other people who were coping with losing loved ones was powerful. He had continued taking the herbs and exercising. After his treatment I taught him the meditation for the metal element.

When I saw Dennis a week later it seemed clear that, while he was still deeply sad over losing his wife, he was on the road to recovery. He continued going to the support group, taking his herbs, and exercising. He found the meditation interesting and saw it as a practical tool for taking the first steps toward developing a spiritual life.

I continued to see Dennis, and each time he seemed a little more vital and a little stronger.

Diet

In the autumn, as natural energy begins to move inward, our optimal diet is one of warmth and substance, including such nourishing and substantial foods as stews, meat dishes, and thick soups. By shifting our diet this way, our bodies can prepare themselves for the changing weather of the autumn and winter. Eating more substantial foods has a strengthening and consolidating effect. This helps the energy of the body begin its inward descent. The goal of the autumn diet is to prepare the body for the coming winter by increasing nourishment while letting go of things not aligned with this process.

The food that best exemplifies the autumn season is the root vegetable. Root vegetables are harvested during the autumn as the weather begins to grow colder, and they aid in nourishing and warming the body and the digestive system. They are toning and at the same time gently detoxifying, as shown in Table 11.

Root vegetable	Properties	Actions
Parsnip the	Pungent taste, warm temperature	Tonifies the spleen and stomach, drains dampness, and clears liver and gall bladder.
Potato	Sweet taste, neutral temperature, high in vitamin C	Nourishing to the digestive system in small to medium quantities; neutralizes excessive acid.
Pumpkin and	Sweet and bitter taste, cool temperature	Tonifies and nourishes the digestive system, drains dampness, benefits the pancreas.
Squash	Sweet taste, warm temperature	Strengthens digestive energy in small to medium quantities
Sweet potato	Sweet taste, warm temperature	Strengthens digestive energy in small to medium quantities
Turnip	Pungent, sweet and bitter taste, neutral temp.	Moves chi and blood, drains dampness, improves the appetite, and aids in detoxifying the body.
Yam	Sweet taste, neutral temperature	Tonifies the spleen and stomach, builds chi, detoxifies the body, and tonifies the yin.

Table 11

Another important aspect of the autumn diet is the increase in the amount of overall food intake — especially in the amount of meat and fish. This does not mean it's suddenly acceptable to eat unhealthy foods; rather, we should eat more *healthy*

133

foods. While meat and fish can be extremely toning, we should consume only as much as our digestive systems can handle. For most people, three to six ounces of meat per meal is all that's necessary. Excessive meat burdens the body and makes it unable to accomplish its functions.

The colors associated with autumn are white and gray, symbolic of the lungs' purity. This warns us that the lungs must be protected during the autumn, when the process of inward contraction can easily damage them. As our energy begins to recede, much of its moisture evaporates. The lungs function best in a state of moisture, but with the coming of autumn all things, including essential body fluids, tend to dry out. So it's essential to nourish the lungs and body fluids during autumn.

The best methods of food preparation during this season are those that increase the warmth of the food. Baking and long, slow cooking of soups and stews are ideal for this. When we cook food for a longer period over a low flame its warming properties are enhanced.

The pungent taste is associated with autumn, and it is balanced by the sour taste. As I mentioned previously, pungency has a moving and dispersing effect within the body, while the sour taste has a consolidating and astringing effect. Both tastes are helpful in harmonizing the body with the shifting energy of autumn.

Listed below are some basic food principles for autumn:

1. **Baked root vegetables.** Pick your favorite root vegetables and bake them for thirty to forty-five minutes. Potatoes, sweet potatoes, squash, pumpkin, or a mixture of these will nourish the body and lungs.

2. **Warming soups and stews.** Pick your favorite vegetables, slice them up, and begin your soup. Add meat of some kind: beef, buffalo, chicken, and turkey all make excellent bases for soup. Add your favorite grains to complete the mix. For a little extra kick, try adding some Chinese herbs (see Appendix B).

3. **Warming meats and toning fish dishes.** Meats by their nature are warming

134

and nourishing, but it's important to cook them for longer periods in the fall to enhance their warming tendencies.

Herbal Formula: "Expression"

The Nature's Roar™ custom formula "Expression" harmonizes the lungs and enhances their ability to let go and experience the flow of life. Through building the power of breath and chi, it can aid in increasing wisdom. It also helps the emotions move through the natural cycle of transformation and heals the psyche by activating the release of old emotions or experiences that have become stuck. You can take "Expression" throughout the year to strengthen your lungs, or only take it during the autumn, from September 21 to about December 21, to harmonize your lungs with the downward flow of autumn energy. The formula contains American ginseng, astragalus, asparagus root, schizandra, fritillaria, and platycodon.

Case Study: Lung/Heart

Daniel, age fifty-four, had smoked cigarettes for thirty years. After a minor heart at- tack, he decided it was time to begin taking control of his own health. He began seeing me because he wanted to stop smoking and strengthen his heart. During the first visit, we spent a lot of time talking about general concepts of holistic health. Daniel knew little about the subject and had many questions. Having grown up with a typical "American" diet, he was unfamiliar with much of the terminology I used. I gave him a copy of my manuscript and recommended he read it. I also recommended that he begin taking my herbal formulas "Rhythm," (see page 80) "Expression," and "Freedom." (see page 99). "Rhythm" is designed to open the liver chi; whenever someone is trying to let go of an addictive pattern, it's helpful to keep the liver chi open and flowing. "Expres-

135

sion" strengthens the lungs, and "Freedom" strengthens and regulates the heart. I gave him a treatment and indicated that we would talk more at our next session.

At first I saw Daniel three times a week. Acupuncture can be very helpful for quitting smoking, but the treatment is needed at least three days a week for the first month or so. The next time I saw Daniel he seemed excited and had many questions. But he didn't feel much different. I explained that, while holistic medicine does work, it tends to work slowly and methodically. We spent time discussing his questions, then talked about the basics of a healthy diet. Before he left, I gave him an acupuncture treatment.

At our next session Daniel was basically the same. He came in excited and full of questions. Although he was having strong cravings, he felt the herbs and acupuncture were of definite benefit. He was beginning to make some dietary changes, and told me that both he and his wife were reading my manuscript. I gave him another acupuncture treatment.

Our sessions went on like this for several weeks. Each time he came in we discussed his questions. Each time Daniel reported that his cravings were subsiding. As time went on, I introduced new concepts. After he had made significant dietary changes, we began working on exercise. After he began exercising regularly, we worked on meditation. Each new concept required a new adjustment, but he was determined to build his health and, while he thought some of my recommendations were odd, he stayed with it.

After several months I began seeing Daniel less frequently. His health had improved steadily, and both he and his wife were following the basic guidelines of my book. They had found their own way to make the system work for them. Watching Daniel transform before my eyes was one of the most beautiful experiences I've had as a practitioner. Each time I saw him, he seemed bit more vibrant. He reported that both he and his wife had never felt better in their lives — their overall well-being had

136

improved, their energy was better, they were happier and more active. He also reported improvement in their sex lif. I continue to see Daniel twice every three months.

Exercise

The autumn is a time of new yin, and the basic energetic theme of the season is letting go. Therefore, we alter the exercise program so there's less emphasis on cardio-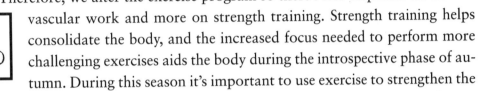vascular work and more on strength training. Strength training helps consolidate the body, and the increased focus needed to perform more challenging exercises aids the body during the introspective phase of autumn. During this season it's important to use exercise to strengthen the power of your lungs. You accomplish this by performing exercises that are shorter and more explosive. Whatever exercise you choose, decrease the amount of time you spend working out and increase the intensity of each workout. Weight lifters should begin to increase the weights they use and decrease the number of repetitions. Shifting the workout in this way helps the lungs grow stronger while helping the body put on more weight in preparation for the winter.

Exercise	Modifications for autumn
Hiking	Hike steeper trails and shorter distances.
Marital arts	Concentrate on speed, quickness, and power of movement.
Weight lifting	Use fewer repetitions and more weight.
Running	Run shorter distances at faster speeds.

Chi Kung

During autumn it's best to use chi kung as a tool for opening and strengthening the lungs and chest, while at the same time cultivating the ability to let go of what is not

necessary in your life. The basic nei kung posture for autumn begins with the basic posture (see Figure 19). The arms, however, are rounded, at the level of the shoulders, with the palms facing the lungs. The hands are nine to twelve inches apart as the exercise begins. Allow the thumb and index fingers to touch. The lung and large intestine meridians pass through the thumb and index fingers, so connecting those fingers will help the chi to move with more focus through those two meridians. Breathe in through the nose and out through the mouth (cleansing breath). Your tongue should touch the roof of the mouth on the inhale, and release on the exhale. This

Figure 19

cleansing breath aids in clearing excess, stagnant, or blocked energy from your lungs and the body. Keep your eyes slightly open, and fix your gaze on the space between your fingers.

The chi kung exercise for the autumn begins in the basic nei kung posture (see Figure 20). With the first inhale, raise your hands up and away from your body, directly in front of the body, remaining shoulder width

Figure 20

apart. Raise them all the way to the level of your shoulders, so that they are straight out in front of your body at shoulder level. Then move your hands straight in to the shoulders, with the palms facing down. When your hands almost reach your shoulders, begin to exhale. Move your hands down your torso, with the palms opening to face straight out away from your body. Your exhale ends when your hands reach their starting position. Do as many repetitions as time permits.

The pace of the exercise is slow and steady. In breathing for this exercise, inhale through your nose with your tongue touching the roof of your mouth, and exhale through your mouth as you release your tongue (cleansing breath).

Journaling

The metal element is involved with release and the ability to let go of things that no longer serve you. The metal element often clarifies who we truly are. As you continue the process of journaling, you will be actively working with metal energy. In this part of the cycle it's common to encounter depression, lethargy, melancholy, repetitive patterns, and an inability to let go of thoughts, feelings, emotions, or experiences from the past. As you begin to express whatever issues are present, you will begin to dissolve such things as your ability to be centered in the present, to move through difficult or traumatic aspects of life, and to move forward, free from the past. This part of the cycle can be especially challenging as you face deeply held feelings. It may seem that the patterns you find cannot be changed, but I assure you that, with diligence and consistency, even the most frightening and deeply held patterns can be observed, interacted with, and eventually expressed. Don't expect that such entrenched patterns will be expressed overnight, but continue to be gentle and compassionate with yourself and allow the process to unfold naturally.

As you feel ready, allow yourself to become aware of your depressive phase.

What does it feel like to be depressed? Allow yourself to describe it in whatever detail comes to you — perhaps colors, shapes, sounds, textures, or scenes. Just write whatever comes, without censoring yourself. Ask yourself what you gain by staying depressed. What do you not have to deal with or face? Ask your depression what it is seeking, what it needs. What do you need to let go of the depression?

Ask yourself these kinds of questions about whatever issues you find. Remember that the goal is to express whatever comes to you. There is nothing that's "supposed" to happen — so allow yourself to truthfully express what you observe.

Meditation

The meditation for autumn is best done in either a traditional seated posture or while walking. Breathe in through the nose with your tongue touching the roof of your mouth, and out through your mouth with the tongue releasing (cleansing breath). This meditation uses the deer exercise (see Chapter 9, page 143) to strengthen the lungs. Take shorter yet more powerful burst-like inhales, and apply the contraction phase of the deer exercise. Then release longer, slower exhales while applying the releasing phase of the deer exercise. Keep your eyes slightly open and your gaze fixed on one object. This meditation is designed to strengthen the lungs and help the body take powerful breaths. With time and regular practice, you can use it to cleanse your lungs and emotions. As with the other meditations, keep your journal close by and write down any thoughts or feelings that emerge. Practice for as long as time permits.

Chapter 9

Winter

Winter is the time of death, withdrawal, and finalization—the time when nature retreats into slumber and returns to its deepest source. It is the season in which our survival depends on properly stored food and other essentials. Trees become barren, animals hibernate, and we return to our core energy and have the opportunity to strengthen our vitality at its deepest level. Winter is symbolized within the five phases by the energy of water. Water, the power of completing the circle of life, is a profound energy that circulates from within the depths of our being.

In general, winter is the time when natural energy moves downward and inward to its deepest point. During this period we move to our most introspective state and face our deepest feelings. It is this season that we spend the rest of the year preparing for, or recovering from. Winter often presents enormous challenges that we must overcome if our life is to continue.

The Kidneys, the Bladder, and the Water Element

According to Chinese philosophy, the organ systems most related to winter and the water element are the kidneys (yin) and the urinary bladder (yang). The kidney system is a vast network responsible for much more than the renal functions we associate with the kidneys in the West. According to TCM, the kidney system, the deepest organ system in the body, is the root of life, as it stores the primal life force known as *jing*, or prenatal chi. The jing and kidney energy are the foundation of the body's vital force. Every organ system, every metabolic activity, and every structure in the body needs jing to survive. When there is no more jing in the body, death ensues.

The jing is divided into yin (substance) and yang (functionality). The *yin jing*, often referred to as *kidney yin*, is the actual substance of life. It is expressed as the sexual fluids and secretions, the cerebrospinal fluids, and the fluids of the endocrine system. A bit of the yin jing goes into every physical structure in the body. The *yang jing*, often referred to as *kidney yang*, is the primal fire that powers every metabolic function in the body. It is the power of the creative and reproductive energies. It's also the power that allows the various aspects of our body, mind, and spirit to grow and develop. Paradoxically, contained within the element of death and completion is the very energy that allows life to exist. People in the West are often taught that life comes from — or exists because of — God. The Chinese take a similar view, although their terminology is different. Their understanding is that the jing has been passed down through the eons from the beginning of creation. So the jing contained within each of us is actually the original energy of creation.

The kidney system rules the physical structures of the body, including the skeleton, bone marrow, lower back, knees, ankles, teeth, hair on the head, brain and mind, and hearing. The system plays an important role in the overall health of the immune system, the digestive system, the endocrine system, and many other vital systems in the body. If the kidney energy is strong, the body and all its systems and functions will be robust. However, if the kidney energy is compromised, the body will tend toward weakness, health problems, chronic illness, low creative and reproductive energy, diminished mental powers, and even mental retardation.

The kidney system rules growth and development. At the moment of conception, jing is transferred from the mother and father to the fetus. From this point on, the quantity and quality of the baby's jing dictates its growth and development. If the child has received strong jing, the processes of growth and development will go smoothly and the baby will be healthy and vigorous. If, however, the jing is compromised in some way, the baby might have developmental difficulties or be born prematurely or underweight. In extreme cases, the child might have some form of birth defect or retardation.

The bladder system is responsible for the excretion of urine. Urine, formed in the kidneys, is a compilation of the fluids left over from the digestive process. When the bladder is weakened or not functioning well, a person may experience difficulty urinating, excess urination, dribbling, incontinence, burning, blockage, or pain.

Positive emotions corresponding to the kidneys are related to will and courage. When the kidneys are strong and jing is abundant, we have feelings of courage and strength. Negative emotions associated with the kidneys are fear and fright. When the kidneys are deficient or not functioning well, we tend to be overly cautious and to avoid situations that are challenging or potentially dangerous.

When our kidney energy is healthy, our bodies and all of their systems and functions will be strong and vibrant. The body, mind, and spirit will possess the power and courage to face any of life's challenges. When our kidney energy is weakened, our bodies and all of their systems and functions will be less vital and more prone to sickness or *dis*-ease, and we may react out of fear when faced with life's challenges.

The kidneys prefer to be in a state of slight warmth with an abundance of yin and yang. One of the kidneys' natural responsibilities is to process fluids. If there is

143

an excessive amount of fluid to process, the kidneys become overburdened. When this condition becomes pathological, it is known as *dampness*. The kidneys also are affected by extremes of heat or cold.

The kidney system is weakened by excessive lifestyle habits, including stress, alcohol and drugs use, lack of sleep, overwork, excessive physical exercise, and especially excessive sexual behavior. Every time a man ejaculates he loses a little bit of jing. A woman, however, is strengthened slightly by an orgasm. But when a woman gives birth to a child, she loses a tremendous amount of jing. It is particularly important to replenish the kidney energy after sex for men and after childbirth for women.

Guarding, maintaining, and refining the jing is a large part of Chinese medicine and seasonal harmony. In fact, much of Taoist alchemy is based on breathing techniques, herbal remedies, and meditations that protect, build, and enhance the jing.

One of these is the *deer exercise*. This involves the contraction and release of the muscles of the uro-genital diaphragm. These include the anus and all the muscles of the genitals. With each inhalation, you tighten and contract these muscles as if you were pulling them up the spine. As you exhale, release the muscles. It's important to have both a strong contraction and a full release and expansion. This is the basic version.

As your muscular control improves, you can move on to the intermediate version. This involves doing a full breathing cycle in each position. For example, inhale, contract and hold the muscles, then exhale without releasing. Inhale again and on the second exhale release the muscles. Insert the same full breathing cycle on the release. For example, exhale and release the muscles, then inhale deeply into the lower abdomen and allow the uro-genital diaphragm to expand like a balloon. Exhale again and, on the second inhale, contract the muscles and pull them up toward the spine.

The advanced form of the deer exercise involves using the breath, the muscular contraction, and a visualization to move energy up the spine, over your head, and

144

down the front of your body. First, inhale, contract the muscles, and visualize sexual energy moving up your spine and over your head to your upper mouth. Then exhale, release the contraction, and visualize the energy moving through your tongue, which is touching the roof of your mouth, and down the front of your body.

The deer exercise — basic, intermediate, or advanced — can be added to most chi kung, nei kung, and meditation exercises to enhance their effectiveness. It's also used to build and strengthen the sexual energy. Consistent practice can increase sexual prowess, enhance stamina, and intensify orgasm.

Tools for Winter

During the winter we move to the deepest and most introspective aspect of our selves. Now is the time to cultivate stillness and knowledge of the true self, the *shen*. While summer is the time for opening the shen, winter is the time for seeing it clearly and accurately. It's a time to come in contact with the deepest feelings and passions we have as human beings, the time we discover what truly moves and motivates us. Winter provides the stillness in which we can peer into the pool of our unconscious mind to discover the secrets preserved there, waiting for our retrieval.

In the movie *The Empire Strikes Back* is a scene that illustrates the psychological aspect of the water element. Luke has gone to the Dego Ba System to train in the Jedi arts with master Yoda. One day during training they stop outside a cave, and Luke sees Yoda making strange facial expressions and postures. Yoda tells him that the cave is a powerful place for the dark side of the force, and says Luke must go in. When Luke goes to pick up his weapons, Yoda say he will not need them, but Luke takes them anyway. Luke asks Yoda what is in the cave, and Yoda tells him only what he brings in with him. As he enters the cave, he sees Darth Vader emerge from the shadows. Both ignite their light sabers and begin to duel. Eventually Luke deals the final blow. He sees Darth Vader's head on the ground, and as the smoke clears he sees his own face in the black helmet.

The story is an allegory about facing our deepest fears to build our will power. Luke's training has come to a pinnacle, so Yoda sends him into the "dark place" to face his "demons." He begins to fight against his manifested dark side. But upon apparent victory, he sees that he has actually lost. He learns he cannot attack his dark side, but must instead remain calm and balanced in the face of terror. By giving in to his fear he becomes engulfed by it.

This story teaches us the power of facing our deepest selves with compassion and tenderness. The dark aspects of our psyche are vital parts of us that we cannot cut off, attack or erase. It is more effective to face our fears with the respect and depth of understanding they deserve. In the deep places within we find the primordial aspects of our true selves. Those deep places hold tremendous power and wisdom, but if we are to gain access to them we must journey to the dark places within ourselves and emerge humbled and renewed.

Winter is also the time when we can tone our bodies at their deepest levels, and strengthen and refine our jing at its source. So with the arrival of winter, it's wise to spend time each day cultivating your jing and refining the stillness of your mind, body, and spirit.

Case Study: Kidneys

Margaret, age thirty-four, came to me because she wanted to get pregnant. She and her husband had been trying for about six months to conceive. It was fortuitous that they came in the middle of autumn. I explained the basic concepts of seasonal harmony, and suggested they follow the guidelines laid out in this book. They started with diet and herbs. I had both Margaret and her husband eat the winter diet and take my herbal formula "Creation" (see page 150) I suggested that they try to just enjoy making love together, without thinking about getting pregnant. The best thing, I indicated, would be to just let it happen. I also gave her an acupuncture treatment to increase the flow of energy through the reproductive areas.

At our next session Margaret said that after taking the herbs and eating the diet for two weeks she felt a little stronger. I recommended she stay on course and continue to build deep strength within her kidneys.

Two weeks later when I saw her, she again reported feeling a bit stronger. I suggested that she and her husband begin doing the chi kung exercises for the water element. I also recommended that they modify their exercise programs according to the principles for the winter.

When she came back two weeks later, Margaret reported more gains in strength, along with a sense of warmth deep inside. She said the chi kung seemed to be helping.

I continued seeing Margaret throughout the winter, and after several months she became pregnant. Nine months later, she delivered a healthy, seven-pound boy.

Diet

The winter and autumn diets are similar, but cold weather requires eating more warming and nourishing food. Because of winter's intensity, it's also wise to consume more food than at any other time of the year. We do this to nourish and strengthen the jing and to sustain our bodies through the winter months. It is *not* a license to eat junk food; rather, we should eat more healthy, nourishing foods.

The foods most representative of winter are meat and fish. In general, meat and fish are tonifying, nourishing, and warming to the body; and in autumn and winter it's important to allow these foods to make up a larger proportion of our diet. Beef, buffalo, chicken, lamb, and turkey are more tonifyng than fish. Of the meats, beef, buffalo, and lamb are the most nourishing and tonifyng, but

147

they also have the highest tendency to cause stagnation. Chicken and turkey are also tonifyng, although less so than red meat. Fish, although less tonifying, is lighter and easier to digest. Eating fish throughout the year is a good idea, because it is a well-balanced food source. The general rule with fish is that the colder the water it lived in, the more tonifyng it will be. But this is not a hard and fast rule, as most fish have similar actions within the body.

Make sure that the meat and fish you consume are natural and free from antibiotics, steroids, and other synthetic additives. Do your best to avoid meat that has been irradiated or chemically treated in any way. If possible, you should eat only natural, free-range meat, and fish that has been caught in clean waters. Several kinds of meat and fish, along with their actions on the body, are listed in Table 12.

Kind of meat/fish	Properties	Action
Ahi tuna nourishes	Sweet taste, mildly warm temperature	Tonifies the spleen, builds chi and body fluids, and the yin.
Albacore tuna nourishes	Sweet taste, mildly warm temperature	Tonifies the spleen, builds chi and body fluids, and the yin.
Beef	Sweet taste, warm temperature	Tonifies the spleen and stomach, builds flesh, drains dampness, and strengthens the bones and muscles. Beef is best eaten in small to medium quantities, as it is very toning and has a tendency to create stagnation.
Buffalo	Sweet taste, warm temperature	Tonifies the spleen, nourishes the flesh, builds muscles, and strengthens bones and chi. Buffalo similar to beef, although it is leaner and has less tendency to stagnate.
Chicken	Sweet taste, warm temperature	Tonifies the flesh, strengthens the liver and the tendons, builds chi, and nourishes the yin.

Table 12

Kind of meat/fish	Properties	Action
Duck	Sweet taste, neutral temperature	Builds the yin, nourishes the stomach, and heals the lungs
Eggs	Sweet taste, neutral temperature	Tonifies the yin, builds fluids, replenishes the essence.
Lamb	Sweet taste, hot temperature	Invigorates the appetite, warms the yang, strongly tonifies the chi, and promotes lactation.
Mackerel	Sweet taste, neutral temperature	Transforms damp, builds the yin, moisturizes and lubricates the flesh, and tonifies chi.
Red snapper	Sweet taste, warm temperature	Tonifies the spleen and tonifies chi.
Salmon ness,	Sweet taste, warm temperature	Tonifies the spleen and stomach, transforms damp-builds muscle and flesh, and nourishes tissue.
Sea bass	Sweet taste, neutral temperature	Tonifies chi, nourishes the yin, and moisturizes tissue.
Shark	Sweet and salty taste, neutral temperature	Tonifies chi and builds muscle and flesh.
Trout	Sweet and sour taste, neutral temperature	Tonifies chi and blood and builds muscle and flesh.
Turkey	Sweet taste, mildly warm temperature	Nourishes the yin and body fluids, builds chi and blood, and benefits the flesh.
Venison	Sweet taste, warm temperature	Tonifies the spleen, builds chi, nourishes the flesh, and invigorates the yang.
Yellowtail tuna	Sweet taste, mildly warm temperature	Tonifies chi and blood, nourishes the yin and fluids, supports the muscle and flesh.

Table 12, continued

149

Winter is the end of the yearly cycle, the time that we use diet to build internal warmth and powerful nourishment. Now is the time to eat larger meals made up of deeply nourishing foods. Rich, nourishing foods may add a few pounds to the body, but that is as it should be — the body is designed to be slightly heavier in winter. Through the process of spring cleansing, you will naturally shed the extra pounds. It's important to allow your body's weight to fluctuate with the seasons. As a culture, we have developed some unnatural ideas about how our bodies should look. In reality, our bodies *should* have more mass in the autumn and winter and be slimmer during the spring and summer. By shifting our attitudes about beauty, we can develop a healthy appreciation for beauty in its natural state.

The color associated with the element of water is dark blue or black. In Chinese thought, black is the most yin of all colors, symbolic of the internal nature of the winter season. During winter it's a good idea to add seaweed and sea vegetables to the diet. These are dark in color and salty in taste. They nourish the kidneys and help the body to harmonize with the depth of winter. Seaweed and sea vegetables can be mixed into soups, baked, added to grains, or steamed. Before baking or steaming, you should wash them, then add them to the mix.

One of the most important things we can do during winter is maintain the warmth of our bodies and protect them from cold. We do this, in part, by avoiding eating anything frozen or excessively cold. If you must eat something cold, be sure to follow it with a warming tea or soup. Food preparation methods in winter are similar to those in autumn, except that in winter you should cook food slightly longer and put more emphasis on enhancing its warming tendencies.

According to TCM, the salty taste corresponds to winter and water. It is balanced by the bitter taste. The salty taste nourishes the kidneys, clears excessive or pathogenic fire, tonifies and consolidates yin, and dissolves nodules or accumulations. Instead of using table salt, try using sea salt, as it is more balanced. While salt is beneficial in small amounts, large amounts can be unbalancing. Salt use depends on the individual, but a good rule of thumb is this: If the taste of the salt dominates the food, you're using too much salt. It's important to balance the salty taste by adding some foods with the bitter taste.

Listed below are some basic food principles for winter:

1. **Similar to the autumn diet.** Eat warming soups and stews, nourishing meat and fish dishes, root vegetables, and warming teas.
2. **Include seaweed and or sea vegetables.** Their salty, nourishing energy helps the body to harmonize with the seasons and is deeply toning to the kidneys.

Herbal Formula: "Creation"

The Nature's Roar™ custom formula "Creation" is based on an ancient Taoist formula and is designed to build the jing and harmonize the kidney energy system. It can strengthen the lower back, knees, ankles, and the whole body. It also enhances sexual energy, creative energy, the power of the mind, and general physical energy. The best essence tonics of Chinese medicine are contained in this mixture. You can take it throughout the year to strengthen your kidneys, or take it from December 21 to about March 21 to harmonize with the energy of winter. This formula can help your body to replenish and build strong jing energy. It contains deer antler, ho sho wu, lycium, morinda, eucommia, schizandra, dang gui, cistanche, and epimedium.

Case Study: Kidneys

 Herb, age seventy-one, was a successful businessman. His wife had been sick for many years and passed away about two years prior to his visit. He came to see me because he had met a woman he liked, but he was having trouble functioning sexually. The desire was there, but he felt

151

stuck emotionally and was unable to maintain an erection. We talked about the basic concepts of Chinese medicine and how they might work for him. I suggested he begin eating the winter diet of stews, soups, and foods that have been cooked for longer periods of time along with fish, chicken, and a little bit of beef.

I suggested that he take my formulas "Nourishment," (see page 119) "Rhythm," (see page 80) and "Creation." "Nourishment" is designed to strengthen chi and digestion, "Rhythm" opens stagnant chi, and "Creation" strengthens the jing. Building the jing would help build his vitality, strengthen his body, and increase his sexual energy. I suggested that he also go to therapy and talk about his feelings, and that he do some journal writing. This would help him open and release some of his blocked emotions. He was on an exercise program he liked, so I didn't want to disturb it. I gave him an acupuncture treatment.

When I saw Herb the next week, he said he was intrigued by my suggestions. He did not feel much, but he enjoyed coming to see me. He had found a therapist but had not yet had a session. He also had made some of the dietary changes I recommended and had taken the herbs. He had not yet written in his journal. I gave him an acupuncture treatment.

The next week when I saw Herb, he said he thought the program was working. He had been with his lady friend and noticed a marked improvement. This motivated him to make more dietary changes and go for an initial session with the therapist. He continued taking the herbs. I gave him another acupuncture treatment.

The following week Herb reported that it was extremely difficult for him to go to therapy. His generation did not talk about their feelings, he said, but he would continue to make the effort. His lady friend was supportive of the changes he was making, and that meant a lot to him. They had both gotten journals and were spending time together at breakfast writing. He said he missed his wife tremendously and felt sad that she had suffered so much. I did my best to be supportive, and gave him an acupuncture treatment.

The next week Herb said that the changes were definitely working. He had been with his lady friend several times, and his sexual function had improved quite a bit. He continued with everything he was doing. I gave him an acupuncture treatment.

I continued to see Herb once a week, and he told me he looked forward to our time together. He even began to bring his lady friend so she could get treatments. He continued with psychotherapy for a while before finally decided it wasn't for him. He did, however, continue to write in his journal, as he enjoyed doing that with his lady friend. He continued taking the herbs and felt they were really helping. He told me that his sexual energy was now "great." I continue to see Herb.

Exercise

Winter is a time of full yin, and the basic energetic theme of the season is depth and stillness. It is an optimal time to engage in exercises that build deep strength. Adjust your workout to include more exercises that build power and speed, and that are anaerobic (strength-building exercises done for short periods of time). In winter, the body's vital energy is at its deepest level, so we alter the workout and spend less time on it, but work more intensely on physically challenging activities. If you are hiking, for example, spend less time hiking, but pick a route that is steep and challenging. In winter, the empha-

Exercise	Modifications for winter
Hiking	Hike steeper trails for shorter distances.
Marital arts	Concentrate on speed, quickness, and the power of movements.
Weight lifting	Use fewer repetitions and more weight.
Running	Run shorter distances at faster speeds.

sis should be on enhancing focus and will within the body and mind.

Chi Kung

The winter chi kung is designed to work with the deepest energy in the body. All of

the energies in the body are valuable and precious, of course, but the Taoists of old placed a special emphasis on kidney energy. The basic nei kung posture for the winter starts with the basic posture (see Figure 21). The arms, however, are in a different position. In all of the nei kung exercises so far, the arms have been symmetrical; in this posture they are not. Hold one of your arms rounded in front of your body, with the palm facing the body at the level of the *tan tien* (three inches below the navel). Place your other hand on the small of your back, with the palm touching the center of your lower back, the fingers pointing to the ground, and your elbow pointing behind you.

Kidney energy is said to be stored in the tan tien. Literally translated, tan tien

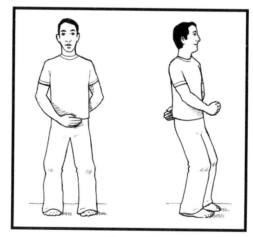

Figure 21

means "elixir field." This is one of the main energy centers in the body. By breathing and focusing energy into this center, we replenish and strengthen our jing. Remember to keep your body relaxed, especially the arm and shoulder that are behind. Breathe in through your nose and out through your nose, with your tongue touching the roof of your mouth. Be sure to spend equal time with each arm in front. Once you become proficient with the basic exercise, add the deer exercise (see page 143). Practice for as long as time permits.

The chi kung exercise for the winter begins with the basic nei kung posture (see Figure 22). The arms are rounded in front of the lower abdomen, palms facing each

other. It's as if your hands are holding a ball of energy throughout the exercise. With the first exhale, bend at the waist, keeping your back straight and your head up, so that your palms follow the course of your legs down toward the feet. As you begin to inhale, move your palms, which are still facing each other, back up the legs until the palms are back in front of your lower abdomen. Make sure the movement is coming from your tan tien and that you are moving through the exercise with a straight back. If you run out of breathing space, simply hold your breath and use earth energy until you get to the end of the movement. The breathing is in through the nose and

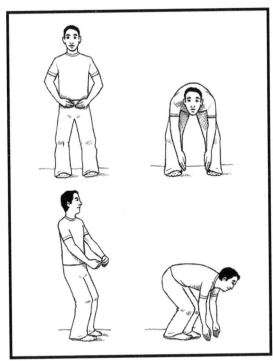

Figure 22

155

out through the nose, with the tongue touching the roof of the mouth. This exercise circulates energy through the kidney meridian, which runs up the insides of the thighs.

The pace of this exercise is deep and slow, like winter itself. Allow yourself to focus on the tan tien. See it glowing brilliantly throughout the exercise. As you become comfortable with the exercise, add the deer exercise. Do as many repetitions as time and your body allow.

Journaling

The water element is the most introverted of the seasonal story. It speaks of moving deep into the core of darkness and stillness. The water energy often reflects the depth of will and power stored within. This final phase of the journaling process is when you are actively working with water energy. In this part of the cycle, it's common to find fears and issues that seem too scary to bring into the light of awareness. As you face and express whatever issues you find, however, you'll begin to uncover your underlying courage, strength, will, and power. You will face what might seem to be the most difficult issues. You are now journeying to the depths of your being to express fears that may be old and painful. *Do not give up.* Keep writing about whatever comes to you. Allow yourself to move slowly; if you need a break, give yourself one. Don't stray far, however, as you have worked hard to get to this point. Don't allow yourself to avoid facing your deepest fears. While the process may be difficult, it offers the greatest and most satisfying rewards.

As you feel ready, allow yourself to observe something you are afraid of. See what it feels like to live with the fear. Notice how it influences your decision-making process, and how it is involved in your life. Ask the fear what it is afraid of and what it needs. What does the fear need to say or express? Do your best to simply write what you become aware of without censoring the process. What do you gain by living with the fear? What do you need to let go of it?

Although the water element is the final phase of the cycle, the cycle never really ends. It just continues anew with the coming of the wood element. So allow yourself to spend whatever time you need in the deep, dark, quiet place of water. Then, when you're ready, allow yourself to be reborn with the coming of the newness of the wood.

Meditation

The meditation for winter is practiced in one of the seated postures, as it involves the cultivation of deep stillness. You should practice this meditation in a quiet setting. Early morning or late night are best. Place your hands on your lower abdomen, with the palms facing your body. Alternate between right over left and vice versa to keep the energy balanced. Breathe in and out through the nose, with your tongue touching the roof of your mouth. Keep your eyes closed and allow your mind to contemplate and experience emptiness and quiet. Summon the courage to honestly face your fears. This does not have to be dramatic or shocking; it's a gentle, consistent movement into your depths, rather than a head-first flying leap. Remember, slow and steady wins the race, and keep your journal close at hand.

Appendix A

The Basic Warm-Up Routine and
How to Practice the Chi Kung Exercises as a Set

Before practicing chi kung, it's important to be warmed up and stretched out. You need to open all of the major joints, including the hips, spine, neck, shoulders, elbows, wrists, knees, ankles, and feet. Below is a great basic warm-up routine. Perform each exercise for several minutes until you feel loose and warm. Feel free to add other exercises to this set.

Warm Up 1: Hip Rotations

Stand with your feet facing forward and shoulder-width apart. Place your hands on your hips. Begin by rotating your hips counter-clockwise. Keep your back straight and move from your hips. Repeat the movement several times, then change directions. After you have done both directions, open your feet to one-and-one-half-times shoulder width. Continue the hip rotations. In this variation allow your hips to move in a bigger circle so that your legs and lower abdomen get stretched as well. Repeat the movement several times, then change directions.

Warm Up 2: Gentle Stretches

Begin with your feet a little closer than shoulder-width apart. Inhale and raise your arms in front of you and over your head. Continue until your hands are over your head and you are doing a gentle backbend. The idea is to get a gentle stretch of the hips, abdomen, and front of the neck. Don't go too far!

Pause with your hands over your head for an exhale and inhale. With the next exhale, allow your hands to move down and out in front of your body. At the same time bend forward from the hips and keep your back straight. Only goes as far you comfortably can. This is a gentle stretch — don't hurt yourself! Pause in the forward bend position for an inhale and an exhale. With the next inhale, allow your hands to rise in front of your body until they arrive over your head. Move with your back straight and your head up. Repeat the movement until you are warm and loose.

Warm Up 3: Shoulder Rotations

Stand with your feet facing forward and shoulder-width apart. Inhale and circle your shoulders up and back; as you bring them down, exhale. Repeat several times, then switch directions and repeat several times.

Warm Up 4: Neck Rotations

Stand with your feet facing forward and shoulder-width apart. Exhale and allow your head to come forward. As you inhale, roll your head toward the left shoulder and allow it to continue toward the back. Continue moving your head in a counter-clockwise direction. Exhale as your head begins moving down on the right side. Repeat several times, then switch directions. Remember to be gentle with your head and neck — they're the only ones you've got!

Warm Up 5: Arm Swings

Stand with your feet facing forward and shoulder-width apart. Bend your knees and sink down into your feet. Inhale and raise your arms out to the sides at the level of your shoulders. With the exhale, swing them down so that the right arm comes in front of your body and the left goes behind. This causes your torso to twist to the

159

left. Be sure to keep your knees from rotating as your arms swing back and forth. After you have twisted as far to the left as you can comfortably go, end your exhale. Inhale as you begin twisting back to the starting position.

Now exhale and swing your left arm in front of your body and your right arm behind. This causes the torso to twist to the right. The exhale ends when you have rotated as far as you can comfortably go. Repeat the exercise several times. Allow your arms to be relaxed so the exercise has a fluid quality.

Warm Up 6: The Basic Nei Kung Posture and the Basic Chi Kung Exercise

First, see the chi kung section in Chapter 3. Nei kung, which is traditionally practiced prior to chi kung, is used to build and open the body as a vessel. This allows the chi to flow smoothly through the meridians. It also allows more chi to flow through the body. Begin by practicing the basic nei kung exercise. Practice for as long as time permits. Then proceed to the basic chi kung exercise. Do as many repetitions as possible.

When practicing chi kung, nei kung, and meditation, keep in mind that it's not necessary to practice every exercise every time. In fact, by practicing one or two exercises consistently you can build depth. Depth allows you to gain an intimate relationship with specific energies. Then you can apply the same depth when learning or practicing a new exercise. Don't rush through the exercises. It's far better to do a few exercises slowly and with the proper focus. The exercises described in this book are profound and subtle; be patient with them.

There are many ways to use the chi kung and nei kung exercises you have learned. Below I've described a few of these ways, but they are not set in stone. I encourage you to experiment with them and find the way you enjoy them most.

Just the Earth: All Levels, Especially Beginners

The earth exercise can be practiced throughout the year. It is an excellent exercise to begin with, as it builds a solid foundation. If you are not practicing the earth exercises throughout the year, at least do them for about a week before each equinox or solstice.

Just the Season: All Levels, Especially Beginners

Especially if you're a beginner, focus on the exercises for the season you're in. While you're learning, it's a good idea to spend time on just one chi kung exercise and one nei kung exercise. By doing just the nei kung and chi kung exercise for one season, you will build depth and get a solid knowledge of each energy.

The Full Set: Intermediate and Advanced Practitioners

The full set involves doing all of the nei kung exercises in a row. Start with the spring and proceed through the cycle to summer, earth, autumn, and winter. Spend a few minutes with each one. Then move on to the chi kung exercises, and do them in the same sequence: spring, summer, earth, autumn, and winter. Make sure you spend the same amount of time on each exercise. In between exercises, allow your feet to come together and your hands to drop to your sides. Take three normal breaths before moving to the next exercise.

After you have finished practicing chi kung and nei kung, spend some time practicing the meditation for the season you're in. One of the main original functions of chi kung and nei kung was to make meditation more powerful. If time is short and you can't meditate after you finish practicing, do some meditation before you go to sleep at night.

161

Appendix B

Herbs

The knowledge and use of herbs has an important and well-respected place in Chinese medicine. In fact, herbal therapy was one of the first forms of Chinese medicine; it's also one of the cornerstonifies of seasonal harmony. Most of the herbs described here can be taken every day, all year long. What follows in Table 13 is a list and description of the single herbs found in the formulas discussed in this book.

Herb Names: Common, Pin Yin, & Latin	Properties	Actions
Albizzia Flower, He Huan Hua, Flos Albizziae Jubilrissin	Sweet taste, neutral temperature	Albizzia flower is prized for its ability to help the shen blossom. It calms the heart, promotes the smooth flow of constrained liver chi, and aids in the transformation of unhealthy emotions. It has traditionally been used in formulas to open the heart and aid the process spiritual cultivation.
Angelica Sinensis, Dang Gui, Radix Angelicae Sinensis	Sweet, acrid, and bitter taste; warm temperature	Tonifies and harmonizes the blood, nourishes flesh, builds body fluids, and regulates the menstrual cycle. One of the best blood tonics of Chinese medicine.
Atractylodes, Bai Zhu, Rhizoma Artactylodis Macrocephalae	Bitter and sweet taste, warm temperature	Tonifies the stomach and spleen, builds muscle mass and strength, nourishes flesh, tonifies the digestive process, and builds energy and endurance. Atractylodes has been a traditional favorite of martial artists, as it builds muscular strength and physical power.
Asparagus Root, Tian Men Dong, Tuber Asparagi Cochinchinesis	Sweet and bitter taste, cold temperature	Tonifies the lungs and kidneys, builds body fluids, moisturizes flesh, and soothes the shen. Asparagus root, especially when wild, is prized for its ability to aid the shen in opening.
Astragalus, Huang Chi, Radix Astragali Membranaceus	Sweet taste, warm temperature	Deeply tonifies the chi, the spleen, the stomach, and the lungs. Tonifies the immune system and the wei chi. Supports the upright energy of the spleen, tonifies the blood, and builds energy and endurance. Astragalus has traditionally been used as a powerful chi and immune system tonic. Used often after childbirth or surgery to speed the healing process.

163

Bupleurum, Chai Hu, Radix Bupleuri	Bitter and acrid taste, cool temperature	Harmonizes and detoxifies the liver and smoothes the flow of liver chi. Calms the mind and emotions, relieves stagnation of chi and blood, calms tension, and harmonizes the digestive process. Bulpeurum traditionally has been used to move and harmonize liver chi.
Codonopsis, Dang Shen, Radix Codonopsitis Pilosulae	Sweet taste, neutral temperature	Tonifies the spleen, stomach, and lungs. Gently tonifies chi and blood, builds body fluids, and nourishes the body. Codonopsis often is referred to as poor man's ginseng or woman's ginseng. It is much less expensive than ginseng, and its effects are similar. However, it's a little milder than ginseng.
Deer Antler, Lu Rong, Cornu Cervi Parvum	Sweet and salty taste, warm temperature	Deeply tonifies the essence, tonifies kidney yang, replenishes marrow. Strengthens bones, the lower back, and the knees. Strengthens sexual energy and function, and enhances sexual vigor, endurance, and vitality. Deer antler is the premier yang jing tonic of Chinese herbal therapy. It has been among the most prized herbs in China for thousands of years. Traditionally, it was available only to emperors because it was so expensive and difficult to obtain. Most of the active ingredients of the deer antler are found in the tip or new growth area. The middle portion and base contain little of the active ingredients and are basically worthless. When the deer's antlers are cut off, they grow back. Consuming extract of deer antler tips imbues the body with the power of regeneration. Deer are not harmed in the process of removing their antlers.
Eucommia, Du Zhong, Cortex Eucommiae Ulmoidis	Sweet and acrid taste, warm temperature	Tonifies the liver and kidneys. Strengthens the body and the yang. Eucommia is the main herb used for strengthening the back, joints, tendons, ligaments, and all connective tissue. It enhances vitality and endurance within the body. This herb traditionally has been a favorite of martial artists because it aids in strengthening and healing the physical frame of the body.

Fritillaria, Chuan Bei Mu, Bulbus Fritillaria Cirrhosae	Bitter and sweet taste, cool temperature	Tonifies and moistens the lungs and transforms phlegm. Fritillaria traditionally is used to cool, nourish, and strengthen the lungs while transforming excess phlegm.
Ginger, Sheng Jiang, Rhizoma Zingiberis Officianlis	Acrid taste, warm temperature	Tonifies the stomach and spleen and soothes the digestive process. Ginger is said to settle a restless stomach and calm a nervous gastrointestinal system. It also has the ability to tone the immune system, in that it harmonizes and strengthens the wei chi. Ginger traditionally is used in conditions of stomach and earth energy imbalance such as diarrhea, vomiting, upset stomach, stomach flu, and cold in the stomach.

Ginseng Ginseng is actually a category of several herbs from the ginseng family. The various kinds of ginseng are excellent herbs. In general, they can be taken every day, and they build health and well-being. It is said that ginseng helps the body adapt to the stresses of life. Ginseng empowers the body to rise to the challenges of life. Remember that better-quality ginseng will have better quantitative and qualitative effects within the body. When ginseng is wild, it is said to have especially powerful shen opening effects. Wild ginseng has been one of the most prized herbs throughout China's history. For this reason it is expensive. Wild ginseng is said to be worth its weight in gold, and it is.

Chinese Red Ginseng, Ren Shen, Radix Ginseng	Sweet and bitter taste, warm temperature	Typically what is considered ginseng. Tonifies chi and builds blood. Strengthens the spleen, stomach, and lungs. Promotes vitality and endurance. Warms the body and improves circulation. Red ginseng can be very warming, so people with underlying heat conditions should be cautious with its consumption.
Korean Red Ginseng, Ren Shen, Radix Ginseng	Sweet and bitter taste, hot temperature	The hottest and most yang form of ginseng. Tonifies the spleen, stomach, and lungs. Invigorates the yang chi and vitalizes the body. It's wise to take small doses of Korean ginseng, as it is tremendously warming and vitalizing. If too much Korean ginseng is taken, it has the tendency to consume yin, overheat the chi, promote excess fire within the body, and create stagnation.

165

American Ginseng, Xi Yang Shen, Radix, Panacis Quinquefolli	Sweet and bitter taste, cool temperature	Tonifies the spleen, stomach, and lungs. Nourishes chi, builds yin and body fluids, strengthens the lungs, and builds vitality and stamina. Does not overheat the chi. American ginseng is the most suitable form for women to consume. It gently tonifies and nourishes the chi and does not consume precious yin and blood as the hotter forms of ginseng do.
Siberian Ginseng, Wu Jia Pi, Cortex Acanthopanacis	Acrid and bitter taste, warm temperature	Tonifies the spleen, kidneys, and lungs. Aids the body in oxygenating blood, increases endurance and stamina, strengthens the heart, supports adrenal energy, and generally tonifies chi. Siberian ginseng is safe to take, as it is only slightly warming and does not overwhelm the body. It is most prized for its ability to build physical endurance and mental toughness.
Jujubee Dates, Da Zao, Fructus Zizyphi Jujubae	Sweet taste, neutral temperature	Tonifies the stomach and spleen. Said to harmonize and gently tone all the organs in the body. Jujubee dates gently tone the digestive process and aid in the process of building chi.
Licorice, Gan Cao, Radix Glycyrrhizae Uralensis	Sweet taste, neutral temperature	Licorice is said to be the most balancing herb in all of Chinese medicine. It balances and harmonizes all of the organ systems in the body. Its effects are gentle and gradual, working in much in the same way the earth energy flows when it is balanced. It traditionally has been used in formulas to harmonize the effects of all the other herbs.
Longan, Long Yan Rou, Arillus Euphoriae Longanae	Sweet taste, warm temperature	Tonifies the heart blood, calms the shen, builds body fluids, and nourishes the spleen. Longan traditionally has been used in formulas to promote restful sleep and provide the heart with substance so the shen can rest more fully within the body. Longan was prized by the empresses of China for its ability to make the skin glow and to build female sexual energy.

Lycium, Go Qi Zi, Fructus Lycii	Sweet taste, neutral temperature	Tonifies the liver blood and kidney yin, builds blood, and nourishes sexual energy. Lycium often is used with herbs that tone the yang. Lycium is one of the most prized essence tonics of Chinese medicine.
Morinda, Bai Ji Tian, Radix Morindae Officinalis	Sweet and acrid taste, warm temperature	Tonifies kidney yang, supports the jing, strengthens the body and mind, and increases sexual energy and function. Morinda has been prized in Chinese medicine because of its ability to build vitality in a balanced way.
Peony, Bai Shao, Radix Paeoniae Lactiflorae	Bitter and sour taste, cool temperature	Tonifies and regulates blood, nourishes the body, gently relieves excess heat, and slightly astringes the body to keep skin firm and control the flesh. Peony also is prized for its ability to relax muscles. Also harmonizes the menstrual system.
Platycodon, Jie Geng, Radix Platycodi Grandiflori	Bitter and acrid taste, neutral temperature	Opens and clears the lungs and throat, promotes the smooth flow of lung chi, and transforms phlegm. Platycodon traditionally has been used as a "guide herb"—it guides other herbs and energy to flow smoothly through the lungs.
Polygala, Yuan Zhi, Radix Polygalae Tenuifoliae	Bitter and acrid taste, warm temperature	Opens the shen and calms the emotions. Polygala is said to open an energy pathway between the heart system and the kidney system. It is an important herb in many formulas because it can unite the heart and kidneys.
Polygonum, Ho Sho Wu, Radix Polygonatum Multiforum	Bitter, sweet, and pungent taste; warm temperature	Deeply tonifies the jing, kidney yin, and liver blood. Builds and replenishes sexual fluids in both men and women. Ho Sho Wu is one of the most widely used herbs in China. It is famous for its ability to promote the life force and slow the aging process, because of its essence regenerating power. Often used as the base herb in kidney tonic and energy-building formulas.

167

Poria, Fu ling, Sclerotium Poria Cocos	Bland taste, neutral temperature	Tonifies the spleen and stomach, drains dampness from the digestive burning space, and tonifies the digestive process. Gently harmonizes the digestive system by cultivating dry and balanced earth energy. Helps to create a space in which the digestive flame can optimally burn. Poria has been one of the main chi tonics throughout Chinese medical history.
Reishi Mushroom, Ling Zhi, Ganoderma Lucidum	Bitter taste, warm temperature	Reishi is one of the most famous and sought after herbs in Chinese medical history. The Taoist masters of old gave it such distinctive names as "the mushroom of immortality," "the mushroom of good fortune," and "the elixir of longevity." Reishi is both a powerful physical herb and a sublime spiritual herb. It works on the health and well-being of the physical body and opens and purifies the shen. If the immune system is not functioning at full capacity, reishi tonifies the system. If the immune system is functioning excessively, reishi acts to calm the system. It is thus able to aid the immune system in functioning well. Reishi detoxifies the liver and blood, calms the emotions, and soothes the mind. It is said to clarify the mental process and aid in the cultivation of wisdom and psychic awareness. Reishi also is famed for its ability to help spiritual aspirants achieve immortality.
Salvia, Dan Shen, Radix Salviae Miltiorrhizae	Bitter taste, cool temperature	Opens the chest and strengthens the functional activity of the heart system. Moves the chi and blood, especially in the chest. Said to remove stagnation and calm the shen. By activating the chi and blood of the chest, salvia eases the workload of the heart and allows it to function more effectively.

Schizandra, Wu Wei Zi, Fructus Schisandrae Chinensis	Sour, sweet, and salty taste; warm temperature	Tonifies the whole body and deeply strengthens the life force. Schizandra has been famed for its ability to beautify the skin. It was the favorite herb of the female members of China's imperial court. Calms the shen, soothes emotions, and sharpens the mind. Also detoxifies and regulates the liver. Schizandra tonifies the kidneys, strengthens sexual energy and function, and builds sexual endurance and staying power. Solidifies the essence and helps the body in building jing. Schizandra also was famed for its ability to build and replenish sexual fluids in both men and women. It's known as the five-flavor herb and is said to strengthen and harmonize all five elements.
Zizyphus, Suan Zao Ren, Semen Zizyphi Spinosae	Bitter taste, cool temperature	Tonifies heart yin, calms the shen, and smoothes liver chi. Zizyphus traditionally has been used to pacify the shen and cool excessive emotional reactions. It is used in formulas to promote restful sleep.

Index